READY TO STEP INTO A MORE CONSCIOUS CULTURE WITHIN YOUR ORGANIZATION?

An engaged, empowered team leads to
a higher performing company
and transforming your culture
begins with knowing your culture.

Use our **Growmotely Culture Tools** with your team
to gain insights directly from them!

**Invite your entire team for
90 days for FREE
with code:**

CLBOOK9OFF

1. Visit growmotely.com
2. Register your organization
3. Invite your Team Members

    (using the code above for 90 days FREE access)

*Note: Growmotely Culture Tools are charged at just
$9 per team member, per month after trial period ends.*

Praise for

CONSCIOUS
LEADERSHIP

Sarah's leadership is the epitome of balance. Balance of both feminine and masculine, logic and intuition, surrender and heart-led action.

Therefore I could not think of anyone better suited to introduce us all to the concept of conscious leadership, which shares in conjunction with her experiences as an intuitive woman.

This book is for all but particularly for those seeking a deeper alignment with oneself, their teams, and what they wish to bring forth in the world.

—Ren Mathieson, CEO of Grow My Team

We see conforming happen all around us, and it's so easy to get caught up in the downstream flow. Sarah, through the years, has been wisely aware and intent on challenging the norm in all facets of life. Year after year, she's endured the discomfort, criticism, and uncertainty that one must face when striving to reach new levels that will enhance the human experience. This book is just as much about how to get there, as it is about why and what it's like when you do.

—Ken Bianchi, CEO & Founder of Hoptix

Having been a part of this leadership journey with Sarah, while having grown not only personally but applying a lot of what she describes into my own businesses, is testimony that the experiences shared in this book can shift your own leadership style to create a more conscious and heart-led world for yourself and your team.

—Pam Dorf, Founder of Kaiz Consulting and Mr. Jasper Says

CONSCIOUS LEADERSHIP

CONSCIOUS LEADERSHIP

A Journey from
Ego to **Heart**

SARAH HAWLEY

Published by Mandala Tree Press
www.mandalatreepress.com

Paperback ISBN: 978-1-954801-03-5
Hardback ISBN: 978-1-954801-11-0
eBook ISBN: 978-1-954801-04-2

BUS071000 BUSINESS & ECONOMICS / Leadership

Cover design by Lisa Barbee
Edited by Valene Wood, Kaitlin Barwick, and Melissa Miller
Typeset by Kaitlin Barwick

www.consciousleadershipbook.com
www.sarahhawley.life
www.growmotely.com

To my husband, Joe Hawley, without whom I
never would have thought all this worth sharing.
Your unconditional love, support, inspiration,
and encouragement for this project is
a gift I'm incredibly grateful for.

CONTENTS

MY ENTREPRENEURIAL TIMELINE

2009   Launch **Wealth Enhancers** (a private wealth management firm for retirees and pre-retirees), officially open for business early 2010.

2011   Launch **League of Extraordinary Women**, a global community for female entrepreneurs.

2012   Rebrand Wealth Enhancers to **WE Private**, relaunch **Wealth Enhancers** as Australia's first membership-based Millennial-focused financial advisory firm.

Publish *Get Rich Slow* book, and ultimately launch **Get Rich Slow** as an online personal finance course that follows the themes in the book.

2013   Dad passes away, and my ownership of our family financial planning business, **WealthMap**, increases from 15 percent to 57.5 percent. Enter into legal proceedings with Dad's ex-business partners in his other company, Synchron (as executor of his estate).

2014   Launch **Grow My Team**, a recruitment company for global remote staff.

Launch **We Love Numbers**, an online fixed-fee bookkeeping company for start-ups.

Sell **WealthMap**.

2015   Sell **WE Private**.

Settle court case related to Dad's estate. Enter into court case with new owners of **WE Private**.

2016 Move to Colorado and launch **We Love Numbers** in the US. Commence $750K capital raise. Later in the year, decide to "fail" **We Love Numbers** and repay investors in full, due to founder burnout.

Buy out two of three business partners in **Grow My Team.**

2017 Move through marriage breakdown and ultimate divorce.

Run **Wealth Enhancers** full time, and **Grow My Team** and **League of Extraordinary Women** part time.

2018 Settle court case with new owners of **WE Private.**

Sell **Wealth Enhancers** to business partner (ex-husband).

2019 Step into **Grow My Team** full time as CEO, buying out final business partner (ex-husband).

2020 Step down from leadership in **League of Extraordinary Women.**

Raise pre-seed round (32 percent over-subscribed) and launch **Growmotely.com**, commencing build of global remote work technology platform.

FOREWORD

As entrepreneurs, we're responsible for the environment we create for our teams, for our companies, and for those we provide value too. The world we live in operates on commerce, and we, as the leaders of our companies, must evolve and choose a higher way of being that will be an asset to humanity, rather than a detriment to it. It's time we start taking this journey from our EGO to our HEART seriously, especially those of us who are here to create the future *through* the companies we're building.

In her book, *Conscious Leadership*, Sarah Hawley takes us on a journey, through her own experience, of stepping into a new, more conscious way of leadership; by living a life of integrity, bringing more compassion and love into our lives and our businesses, and empowering those we lead to reach for their highest potential.

This journey is not an easy one, it forces us to look in the mirror at ourselves and our own stories, challenging us to look at the way we show up as leaders, and hopefully providing the foundation to do better. In order to make an impact in the world, to really shift the collective narrative, we must first look deep within ourselves and heal the parts of *us* calling out for our attention. The energy we embody pours over into the companies we build and the teams we lead and therefore trickles out into the services or products we provide. As leaders we have a very real opportunity to make a difference and it all starts from within ourselves.

By vulnerably sharing her own experience—both the challenges and the successes, and the many lessons and growth they've provided—Sarah takes us through her own beautiful journey of redefining what it means to be a successful entrepreneur and leader, proving it's not only possible to embody a loving presence in business but it's actually necessary if we're going to evolve as a culture into a new way of being.

I'm so grateful for the presence and growth Sarah has provided me in my own life. I was blessed with the opportunity to quarantine with her during the initial lock down that took place in March 2020. We met at a friend's retreat that took place just a couple of weeks prior and without knowing much about each other decided to see what that initial energetic connection was all about. She came to Austin and we went on our first date right as the world teetered on the brink of disaster! Not knowing what would happen, we took a leap of faith and trusted the path the universe had led us down, quarantining together. Over one year later we're now married with a baby boy on the way. I can't begin to put into words what a transformational experience it has been to be in this woman's presence and the expansive growth it's provided me, not just on my entrepreneurial endeavors but on both a personal and spiritual level as well.

Leadership is something I know quite a bit about, playing professional football in the NFL for eight seasons. I played with some great leaders throughout my career, both coaches and teammates, and as I was just beginning my own journey into entrepreneurship, I was open and eager to learn how to implement my own leadership skills into the business world building a new business and team of my own. There's been no greater teacher to have shown me more about what it truly means to selflessly embody the attributes of a conscious leader than Sarah.

Of course there's a lot of advice someone who's been in business for over seventeen years, successfully founding and exiting multiple seven-figure companies, can provide someone else just starting out on their own journey, and she had plenty of stories to share. Most of these stories have ended up in this book, all of which have impacted my life, and I know, if you stay open, will also have an impact on your journey as well. But the most impactful thing about being with Sarah isn't all of the experience she has; it's the way she's able to fully embody the lessons, growth, and wisdom from her many years of experience. The privilege to witness the way she shows up each day, her ability to constantly question her own stories, overcome her own fears, doubts, limiting beliefs, and worries, always taking the time to see where she can *do*, and more importantly, be better, is truly a sight to behold. The way she leads her teams is incredibly impactful, continually empowering them to reach for their own highest potential.

Sarah's energy, wisdom, and ability to embody conscious leadership has had such a profound impact on my life, and I'm so deeply grateful for everything she's taught me, and most importantly, *shown me*, through her own experience, her wisdom, and her ability to inspire me to work through my own fears, limiting beliefs, and worries, allowing me to step into my own fullest potential.

I have no doubt that by reading this book, she will also inspire you. You'll become a better leader, you'll become a better person, you'll figure out how to embody your own leadership style, develop tools and resources to find a higher level of success, and lastly, you'll be challenged to live a life with more intention and integrity.

We all have an incredible opportunity to step up and lead with a higher sense of awareness, speaking our own truth and being more transparent, empowering others to do the same. This is how we make a difference, this is how we change the world.

With love and gratitude,
Joe Hawley

INTRODUCTION

Straight up. Read this book and toss it if nothing resonates.
This is not a business book on how to be the best leader on the planet. This is simply *my* story and *my* journey to a place of finding *my* personal truth and authenticity as a leader. To a place of finding my personal power as a leader and, as a result, building an empowered and engaged team.

However, it is *my* way, and it's not the only way. In fact, if I were to urge you to do anything at all, it would be to sit with yourself, do your inner work, and get to know yourself. Heal your wounds (we all have them), integrate your shadows (we all have them too), and disarm your ego (we all have one).

Show up with as much of yourself and as little of everyone else as you can.

Emulating great leaders is not how we become great leaders.

Perhaps it's a start, but it'll only take us so far, and it'll see us out of alignment and that misalignment will reflect in the culture of the organizations we lead.

A great leader is a conscious leader, and consciousness by its very definition is awareness of self, awareness of the world around us.

If I were to summarize, or create a definition of, conscious leadership based on everything I learned, experienced, integrated, and practiced, it would go something like this:

1

- Bringing your whole self and embodying authentic vulnerability
- Practicing ownership, self-awareness, and self-reflection
- Operating in alignment and in connection with a higher purpose

Bringing your whole self and embodying authentic vulnerability

We're emerging from years of conditioning that tells us that as leaders we need to show no weakness and distance ourselves from our team. A conscious leader does the opposite. While their function is to keep the team on track, focused, and working toward the vision, they can do this alongside their team, and they can do it from a place of openness. Sharing both their personal and professional struggles as they happen, as well as their victories. Allowing space for them to be seen fully, ultimately creating deeper bonds and connection with the team, and creating space for others to be and bring their whole selves too.

Practicing ownership, self-awareness, and self-reflection

A conscious leader has a well-established and consistent practice of focusing inward through challenges. They ask themselves, "What role have I played in this situation? How can I learn and grow from it?" They build an awareness of who they are as people, identify and understand their triggers, and are always working to bring their unconscious behavior to the light. Conscious leaders seek out feedback and communicate from a place of shared experiences, asking questions and being endlessly curious.

Operating in alignment and in connection with a higher purpose

Leading with consciousness means being aligned with the vision and higher purpose of the organization. This is a genuine feeling of "There's nothing else in this world I'd rather be working toward." It means operating from a place of deep connection with the higher purpose and with one's own intuition. While strategic planning and such tools can and will play a role in moving things forward, conscious leadership involves trusting one's intuition and surrendering to a more fluid process.

The pages of this book contain my personal experiences, woven into stories to illustrate my journey from unconscious leadership to where I find myself today. Leading from a far more connected, self-aware, and vulnerable place.

As an aside, the stories and experiences I've shared will likely resonate more with the entrepreneurs among us—those who have a greater ability to shift and make changes within their organizations (which I understand is not always possible when working as a leader within a large corporation).

I have not personally worked in large companies. I have been a founder for the past ten years, and prior to that, I worked in a family business. It's been a long time since I've had a boss, and I felt it important to frame this up before you dive in.

Either way, I hope you find it useful. Inspiring.

I hope it sparks something in you or resonates in some way.

Most of all, I hope it helps both you and your team experience more joy and fulfilment in the work you do together. Because in the end, what else really matters?

CHAPTER ONE

A COMPANY IS BORN

It was 2011, about a year after I'd started my first real business (a private wealth management firm called WE Private), when three fellow female entrepreneurs and I birthed the League of Extraordinary Women. I use the word "birthed" because that's what it was, and we really didn't know at the time exactly what was about to transpire.

The four of us had met at an event in Melbourne, Australia, the previous year. The event was a large-scale conference for early-stage founders called Unconvention and was run by The Entourage, a newly launched and thriving community of young entrepreneurs, founded by my now dear friend Jack Delosa.

Sheryl (Shez) Thai, Liz Volpe, Marie Cruz, and I had hit it off. We shared the commonality of each being in our first year of business, and we were among the few women regularly attending events and participating in the organization.

We'd catch up for cupcakes and coffee at Shez's cafe, Cupcake Central, and talk business, share stories, and learn from each other.

We'd found our tiny girl tribe and would often lament the fact there were few other women attending business events—and even fewer on stage sharing their stories for us newbies to learn from.

All this was about to change.

The entire landscape for female entrepreneurs in Australia was about to change.

It was Shez who brought the idea to us all. What if we ran a little event, just for women like us? There must be twenty or thirty other women in Melbourne who'd be down to get together? We could find one or two successful female entrepreneurs, have them share their stories, and then create some space for attendees to get to know each other.

We unanimously agreed it'd be worthwhile, even if just for the four of us.

We set to work and decided on a date a few weeks out. We came up with the name League of Extraordinary Women (I've asked my cofounders and none of us can remember where or how our name came about) and threw together a Facebook page with a picture of She-Ra the Princess of Power as the profile picture!

As timing would have it, The Entourage was holding another Unconvention that weekend, and Jack gave us a five-minute slot to jump on stage right before lunch and let the audience know about our event.

Looking back, it feels to me as if the four of us up on stage that day, with Liz hustling the crowd as she does best, was the moment the League was born.

Instantly we knew it was bigger than us. The energy around it was palpable.

Over the coming week or two, we sold 160 tickets and had to switch up our venue at the last minute. I remember sitting in the lounge of my high-rise apartment in Southbank, refreshing our Facebook page to another 100 likes every few minutes. It was insane.

We hadn't even held our first event yet and were receiving emails from women in Sydney, Brisbane, and even New Zealand asking when the League was coming there. To say this was one of the most thrilling times in my entrepreneurial career would be an understatement.

Especially so early on.

I'd been working hard at growing WE Private, the financial advisory practice I was so passionate about, but when it came to building a brand, and traction, and excitement . . . let's just say private wealth management did not have anywhere near the same buzz as did what was happening with the League.

After the success of our inaugural event, upstairs at Little Red Pocket in Melbourne, the League was like a freight train. There was no stopping it. Before long, we'd launched with similar events in Sydney, Brisbane, Adelaide, and Perth. Then came Run the World and Tech Formation, two of Australia's largest conferences for female entrepreneurs, and eventually, the Female Entrepreneurship Awards. We toured the United States in 2016 and held events in San Francisco, New York, and Denver. Along the way, we also supported events in Vancouver, London, and even South Africa.

It's been wild. But one thing stood out to me from day one when I was standing up on stage alongside three of my best friends, and it changed the way I look at business forever: the League has a life of its own.

It's not us—any of the founders.

We were simply the stewards chosen to corral this idea (which mostly meant running behind it frantically, trying to keep up).

The League came through us—it's not of us.

This was my awakening to the concept that a business has a consciousness of its own. It has its own reason for being, its own destiny, and we as the founders, CEOs, or leaders are simply a part of the team working with it to bring it to its fullest potential.

Up to the time of this writing, the League hasn't existed to provide us (the founders) with financial abundance or any such thing. The League was born to play a significant role in changing the game for women in business—not just in Australia but across the globe.

It's been clear all along that that has been its priority and reason for being. The League was birthed to change the unconscious bias that exists in business and to provide a platform for the incredible women who've walked before us to tell their stories. It exists to show the women who start businesses every year that they have just as much opportunity to "make it" as their male counterparts, after all (roughly)

50 percent of all new businesses started in both Australia and the US each year are started by women. Levelling the playing field was (and remains) long overdue.

In 2017, it had been a while since all the founders had attended a Run the World conference, and we decided to make it a big one. I flew back from the United States (where I was living) to ensure we could all be there.

It was an incredible event, but what was *most* incredible was the common theme running through every single speaker's presentation that day:

- Heart-led leadership
- Building companies based on intuition
- Embracing the feminine energy and flow

It was wild. Unplanned. Unexpected. Awe-inspiring.

I know it awakened something in me, something that had been clawing to break free. Something deep inside me that knew there was a better way to lead.

As I sat listening to some of the world's most accomplished female business owners, I, too, received permission to fully bring forth that part of me wanting to shine. That part of me that I had previously dimmed down to survive in the masculine world I'd risen in.

Once again, the League was speaking to us all. Not from *us*, any of the founders, but *to* all of us in the room. The League was making it known the world was now ready for powerful women to soften into their feminine energy, their flow, and their intuitive nature—and to lead in that way. It was telling us to bring both the masculine and feminine energies into balance within the world of business and that we'd be rewarded for it.

It's been these experiences with the League that have opened me up to the fact that I am *not* my company. I am not *any* company. As entrepreneurs, we act as conduits for ideas to flow through, and we work to bring them to life.

The gift in grasping this concept is the freedom it provides for all.

Freedom for the idea to become everything it's meant to be (without the constraints our individual limited thinking might otherwise impose). Freedom for ourselves to enjoy and pursue other interests. Freedom, perhaps, to step aside if another leader may be more appropriate.

When we attach to our businesses in a way where we feel they are a part of us, or an extension of us, it can be very stressful and emotional. If a client is upset, we take it personally; if the business wins an award, we take it personally. These extreme highs and lows take their toll on us personally and professionally and tend to constrain the growth of the business as we become more and more worn down riding the waves.

While it's important to monitor these things as leaders and use them as indicators to continue to guide our businesses in a positive and expansive direction, it's equally important to loosen our grip and trust the natural evolution and consciousness of the business.

Learn to listen and to trust that the business knows where it's meant to go next.

CHAPTER TWO

RETHINKING GOALS

For almost ten years, I followed a fairly rigid business-planning structure to provide momentum and focus for myself and my team. Initially we used the Rockefeller Habits system and ultimately replaced this with Traction, Inc. EOS (the Entrepreneurial Operating System), both popular among members of the global membership group Entrepreneurs' Organization, of which I've been a member since 2013.

I was a huge fan.

Using a system like this gave me a framework to hone and define our bigger picture vision, engage the team, and break everything down into quarterly goals. In a nutshell, it goes like this:

- Create a big picture vision.
- Build a one-year strategic plan.
- Develop 90-day targets and projects.

This system served us well—or so I thought. It certainly gave us something to focus on as a team, and something to do every quarter. It was a chance to reflect and plan, and it did keep us moving forward.

A constant source of frustration, however, was the fact that we rarely (if ever) hit our targets or completed our projects in time. It always baffled me. We'd start out so motivated as a team, rallying around our exciting new projects and growth targets, and then fall flat.

The daily grind would kick back in, most of us would put our projects off until the end of the quarter (myself included), and it would become a sprint to try to complete what we could in a hurry as our 90-day milestone approached. This often resulted in things not being finalized and being pushed into the next quarter.

Looking back now, I don't remember *ever* hitting all our numbers in a quarter. Ever. In ten years.

For a long time, I kept going with this. It still created a sense of momentum, and, for the most part, our businesses grew and expanded along the way anyway, so I didn't give it too much thought. I figured it was what all my peers were doing, and if I kept at it, eventually we'd figure out the puzzle and start hitting targets.

In June 2019, I woke one day with a sense of clarity. It was a hot morning in Tulum, Mexico, and I was spending a couple of weeks down there solo following a summit I'd attended the previous weekend.

It was the day before our quarterly planning session, and, as per my usual structure, I'd blocked my calendar out for the day in order to spend it preparing and figuring out the bones of our quarterly plan ahead of time.

As I lay in bed staring up at the ceiling, I realized none of it made any sense to me anymore. The whole idea of quarterly planning was turned on its head, and my intuition was guiding me to do it a different way.

Planning 90-day projects didn't make sense because *not every project takes 90 days.*

Setting specific goals didn't make sense—especially with ten years of evidence that we never reached them—and it was just leaving us constantly disappointed.

I also explored the notion that perhaps sometimes the company wanted to do *more* than my goal-setting targets allowed for. Why was I anchoring us to something, rather than trusting the organization to go where it needed and wanted to go?

Even writing this now, and imagining you reading it, is bringing me back to that morning and how wild a concept I was conceiving.

As I showered and got ready for my day, I wondered to myself, "Am I just being lazy? Do I just want to spend the day at the beach tomorrow instead of getting the team together to plan?" There was a lot of resistance coming up in me.

The concept I'd woken up with was to relinquish any specific goals and trust us to simply move each day in the direction of our purpose as a company. Releasing the attachment to projects on a 90-day schedule would allow them to be put forward by anyone, at any time, and then let be completed in the appropriate time frame for each individual project.

I rode the push bike I'd rented for my stay to my favorite plant-based cafe and ordered a kombucha. I sat with this idea. Contemplating. Allowing it to feel its way into my being. Getting to know it and getting comfortable with it.

In the end, I made the decision to sleep on it and ask my team what they thought the next day—*if* I woke up still feeling it.

We were just five of us back then, and when I explained my thoughts to the team, we unanimously agreed it felt right and made sense to give it a try.

We held our last formal quarterly planning session that day, closing out the previous quarter and setting forth into a new frontier with a bunch of exciting projects, each with individually estimated timelines and no fixed goals.

While I felt apprehensive, something deep inside me felt aligned. There was a sense of trust in the process and surrender. To ease my nerves, I reminded myself, "What's it all for if not to have a little fun and try new things?"

Our first project was completed two weeks later. It was our new company dashboard, moving from the Google Sheet we'd been using to a software that pulled data from many sources and integrated it all together.

Two new projects were added in its place by our financial controller, one of which she also completed in just a few weeks.

You get the idea.

My hunch was right. When we weren't anchored to a 90-day time frame, we were able to achieve more of what actually needed to be achieved and in a more realistic time frame. Which also means including projects that take longer than 90 days, things we no longer need to feel as though we're failing or falling behind because they couldn't get done in time.

This whole exercise moved us into a more fluid planning momentum and put more power and autonomy into the hands of each team member.

What it looks like presently:

- Anyone can propose a project at any time. A project is something that sits outside of our day-to-day operations and will improve the business in some way. It could be a new service offering, an improved process, a government grant we're applying for, etc. It's something that may need more than one person's involvement, and it usually takes some coordination, planning, and monitoring in order to see it to completion.
- Provided everyone agrees the project is worthy (some refining may occur), it is added to our weekly meeting slide deck with a project owner, estimated completion date, and a description of what it will look like upon completion. Then, each week, the project owner will give a status report on the project and let the team know if they are stuck on anything and need help.

- Anyone can propose and own a project and ask for volunteers to help get it completed. We usually have five to seven projects running at a time, depending on how busy we are. With an engaged and empowered team, there always seems to be things being put forward.

- When the project is completed, we congratulate the owner and celebrate!

What I enjoy most about this shift is the fluid energy and the surrender I'm able to embrace as the leader. The more empowered we all are to *listen* to the company, and act on what we hear, the more we seem to achieve.

CHAPTER THREE

THE ONLY SCORE
THAT MATTERS

I remember clearly the first time I asked my team how happy they were. I remember because there was a lot going on inside of me in the lead up to asking this simple anonymous question.

How happy are you at work?

I had come back from my first year of the Entrepreneurial Master's Program at MIT in Boston brimming with ideas. One idea was to improve our culture. Knowing we had to get an idea of where we were starting meant asking the team and getting the truth out of them.

My truth was that I'd been living in a bubble. We had a super cool office in South Melbourne, Australia. It was a terrace house that backed onto a laneway. We'd throw open the garage and host epic parties with DJs, kegs, and beer pong for our community. It was a fun place to work, no doubt, and looked more like a creative studio than a financial planning office.

But I knew in my heart our culture wasn't totally healthy. There was some rot in there, and I needed to understand it.

Of course, knowing that and bringing myself around to facing it was another thing. I'd been externally focused for so long, looking at how shiny it all appeared from the outside—it was scary for me to really look internally.

There's no question we'd been trying hard to create a positive culture, but there was also no question we had continual, high staff turnover and a track record of attracting great people into the business only for them to turn around about three months later and head back to the corporate world, disillusioned.

Irrespective of how fantastic it looked from the outside, it was just appearances, and the brand and the office and all the fanfare wasn't making my people happy. Hell, it wasn't making *me* happy.

Before asking them, I remember predicting what they'd say. I remember thinking how ungrateful they were, and how misunderstood I was. I was doing so much for them, and yet they *still* weren't happy.

My goodness, it makes me feel ill now to think of my mental patterning!

I was scared, and fear will drive us in one of two directions: into and through the fire, or as far away from it as possible.

Thankfully, I've always been a sucker for walking through that fire, so I followed my intuition to ask the question and make a start toward building a happy, thriving team who loved working together each day.

It's interesting to think I don't even remember now exactly what that first score was, somewhere between a six and a seven (out of ten) roughly, and I also don't remember what the feedback was specifically. What mattered was that I was taking the blinders off and listening to my team. I was listening to what was going on for them, to what mattered, and I was no longer making assumptions and stories in my mind.

At the same time, I took back control of my powerful thoughts and words. I realized that if I continued to complain about my team to anyone who'd listen, and if I continued to think about their incompetence and how ungrateful they were, I'd continue to have that incompetent, ungrateful team.

Our thoughts are our reality.

From that moment forward, I ceased speaking and thinking negatively about my team. If it ever came up in conversation with a fellow entrepreneur, I'd quickly steer our discussions in another direction. Instead, I started speaking into reality the team I wanted. I *now* told anyone who'd listen how much I loved my team, how amazing they were, how talented.

And, importantly, I listened to them. The monthly happiness score became my guidepost for how well I was doing as a leader and how healthy our company culture was.

It still is.

While it's important we have a healthy balance sheet and our profit and loss statement in the black, what really matters long term is how happy we are as a team and how happy our customers are partnering with us.

It occurred to me back then that nothing mattered if the business wasn't making a positive impact in everything it did. Nothing mattered if I wasn't making a positive impact as a leader. Money is meaningless without happiness and peace of mind.

I've never been in it for the money anyway. I'm an entrepreneur because I get obsessed about a problem and can't let it go until I'm working on solving it. I'm an entrepreneur because I love the energy of creation, I love the freedom to work without constraints bringing something new to the world. I'm an entrepreneur because I get huge kicks out of positively impacting the lives of others and being a part of making this world a better place. I want to know I'm a driver for positive change and taking the wheel. It's in my DNA, and the only role money plays in it all is an energy source to harness to bring these ideas and solutions to their fullest and most expansive potential.

It's been over five years now.

Every single month, without fail, I ask the question, *How happy are you at work?* I ask our customers, *How happy are you partnering with us?* And every single week in our All Company meeting, we look at those scores and we review any of the anonymous feedback or comments that have come through.

We discuss the scores and the feedback candidly and make plans to adjust and improve what we're doing. We celebrate the positive remarks, and I—as the captain of the ship—feel confident knowing I have the information I need to navigate our course.

These scores are my leading indicators. I like them to be above 9/10 and if they drop below 8/10, I really dive in. It's cause for concern for me, and it'll be my focus to resolve as quickly as possible.

What I've learned over the years is not to be afraid. I've learned a drop in my team's happiness score is generally a case of misalignment, and open dialogue will either help realign everyone, or provide an opening to part ways in full support of each other. This goes for customers too.

I've also learned that culture has little to do with ping pong tables, fancy offices, or cool parties. It's not to say some of these things won't be appreciated; however, assuming they will be is where we trip up as leaders.

Culture is created through how we show up every day, consistently. It's essentially the values of the organization and the ways in which we work.

As an aside, we began our transition to a fully flexible and fully remote organization not long after I started this open dialogue with my team about what they wanted. It turned out that while to some degree they appreciated the space we had in South Melbourne, they ranked freedom and flexibility higher. Being able to work from home (or wherever really) was far more important to them. Being trusted to work remotely meant the world.

CHAPTER FOUR

RESIGNING AS BOSS

Not too long before I woke up rethinking the way we'd been doing our business planning, I resigned as "boss."

Someone in the team had sent me an email asking if they could take a day off to attend an important event at their son's school. Reading the email, I instantly felt how strange it was for a grown woman to be asking *my* permission to take some time out. A grown woman with a child no less—someone who's potentially far more responsible than I am!

Along with how absurd it felt, I also really didn't have the time or energy to think about whether she *could* take the time off or not.

It didn't feel like a decision I wanted to make. Or needed to make.

This all happened after I'd stepped into Grow My Team full time as CEO. I'd bought out my three former business partners over the years, sold my share in Wealth Enhancers to my ex-husband, Finn Kelly, and was diving headfirst into this struggling little start-up.

It had been some years since I'd had such a small team and been managing people so directly. I guess it was the time and space in between that made me see things differently when I received her email request.

In my body, I felt it: I did not want to "manage" people. I valued my own freedom at this stage too much, and I imagined the people working alongside me would likely value their freedom too.

I called a meeting soon after and resigned as boss.

I let everyone in my little team (I think there were five of us at the time) know I trusted them to manage their own working schedule, their own vacation leave, and any other time off they needed. I also let them know leave was unlimited. If they can make it work, by all means they can take it.

Of course, in the case of an emergency, we'd all pitch in to cover someone so they could focus on what they needed to, but outside of that, for any planned time off, we were on our own to figure out whether we could take the time and how we'd go about getting things done in our absence.

I suggested we could all work among ourselves to have our team-mates cover us if needed and repay the favor when the opportunity later arose. All we needed to do was make sure that we communicated openly and that we each took responsibility for ensuring our job got done.

This included myself.

I was headed to Costa Rica for an Ayahuasca retreat a few weeks later and wanted to completely switch off. I'd arranged for our operations consultant to keep an eye on my emails while I was away and for our financial controller to run the weekly meeting. Everything else I made sure I was on top of as much as I could be before heading out.

I used this example to illustrate how we could work together cohesively and responsibly moving forward.

While it took a little adjusting—mainly for my team to learn to trust themselves and also for them to trust me that I'd meant what I said—we quickly got into a groove and what I've seen and experienced since is a profound level of ownership over the roles each of us play in the organization.

For the most part, we tend to choose to work while we travel rather than having big chunks of time off. However, we have the flexibility to stack our days differently while we're away, and every so often someone takes some days completely offline and we pitch in to cover them.

The other incredible benefit of this way of operating is how much it frees each of us up to bring our best work.

As the CEO, I'm clear on my role—vision, strategy, and leadership.

I also enjoy content creation as a value addition to the marketing team's already rolling strategy. They do not rely on my content to keep telling our brand story, but I'm able to contribute from time to time when inspiration strikes because it's something I love to do.

For me to be free to focus on vision, strategy, and leadership, I don't need to be overseeing and directing everything everyone else is doing. If I'm doing my job in championing the vision, setting the strategy, and leading, my team is able to do their best job handling whatever it is they handle.

In mid-2019, we rebranded Grow My Team.

It was time, leadership had changed, our vision had evolved, and we were embarking on the next phase of the company's growth. Our new head of marketing and brand, Theodora Gatin (who had come across from my previous team at Wealth Enhancers), was now at the helm of telling our story, and she was feeling into what and how the company wanted to come across now.

It was Theo who channeled and created the new brand, it was Theo who worked on it and brought it to life, and it was Theo who presented it to us all during a team meeting when she felt it was ready.

She presented it to me, the CEO, at the same time as she presented it to the rest of the team. I hadn't even seen a sneak preview.

This was a significant moment for me, as I knew I'd finally let go of any last remaining tendencies to need to be involved. I knew I'd come to a place where I'd truly surrendered to trusting my team fully.

We all loved the new brand; it is the perfect expression of who we are as a business now and where we're headed.

I know for Theo it feels good. She fully owns the brand; it's her baby, and she's the one to work with it (and with her team) to continue to bring its voice to the world.

This is empowerment for all of us. We all trust each other to take care of our area of the business, of the parts that we're best equipped to look after. It's also freeing for all of us to know we don't need to worry or get involved in things that are not within our area of expertise.

CHAPTER FIVE

THE VALUE OF VALUES

Several months prior to writing, our operations and finance manager, Apple, had built out some new pricing for one of our services and presented the new model to us in our weekly All Company meeting. Once again, I had no idea this was happening—however, I agreed with it and supported it.

It was well thought out and made sense.

After the meeting, I was in awe thinking about where we'd gotten to, about how empowered and powerful my team had become.

Of course, in big companies, I'd suppose decisions like this are made by heads of department all the time. However, we're a (now) thirteen-person company. A team of people based all over the world, working remotely, some of whom have never met in person.

How had it come to be that my team could confidently take all this decisive action and have me sit there every time thinking, "Yep, that's logical and fair, let's do that"? How was it they were able to innovate and evolve our business in the same ways I would if I were involved in the process?

It's what I'd wanted and what I'd been moving toward for several years. I was grateful it had come to be, and I was curious about how we'd arrived at this place. What exactly was it in how we were operating that made this possible?

Then, it dawned on me.

Every single week at the beginning of our All Company meeting (where the entire team is present on camera), we go through our vision, our purpose, our values, and our brand promises. Every week. Without fail.

When we do this, we tell "values stories"—examples of where we've lived our values, or where a customer has lived a value, or any example we can find of embodying who we are. We also read our vision and purpose, and then we examine our brand promises and discuss any examples of where we've delivered on them or perhaps failed to deliver on them.

This process, it occurred to me, is the reason the team has the confidence they do to make decisions in the way they do. They know to their very core *who* we are, *why* we exist, and *how* we do things.

This may be the most important thing I do as the leader every week.

This is the thing that frees us to be the best we can be in our respective areas, the thing that gives us the confidence to make decisions and act when needed.

Simply put, we're deeply connected with who we are as a business.

The other value of this process and being intimately connected with who and how we are culturally is how easy it becomes to attract and retain team members who will thrive within our organization.

At Grow My Team, one of our core values is "Be flexible and scalable." We are a fast-moving start-up and are constantly evolving our systems and processes as the company expands. Most things we have a framework for, some areas are more built out than others, and all of it is being improved upon weekly. These continual, incremental innovations ensure that what we're building is more flexible than it is rigid and is able to work 10 times, 100 times, or 1,000 times.

This makes for a dynamic working environment, and to enjoy this style of operating, one needs to be comfortable with uncertainty and change and be adaptable and open-minded. It's more suited to those who take a more growth-oriented approach to their careers and like to explore their own potential and possibilities for movement within their roles, and within the organization.

For those who are more comfortable learning a tried and tested way of doing things, and mastering it, they'd likely find our culture uncomfortable.

But this is ultimately what culture is: the daily living out of the values of the organization. And to attract those who'll thrive in our companies, we as leaders need to know who we are. Not who we aspire to be—who we actually are.

There's no point advertising flexibility if the organization is highly structured (or vice versa). Our values are a true reflection of what's important to us, and the clearer I've become about ours over the years, the easier it's been for us to make additions to our team who go on to perform well and love working with us.

CHAPTER SIX

STAY IN YOUR LANE

I t took me many years to understand my areas of genius and to be comfortable and confident enough to stay within those areas.

As a serial entrepreneur who enjoys the role of CEO in a start-up company I've founded, there are three things that form my role:

1. Vision
2. Strategy
3. Leadership

As I mentioned previously, I also really enjoy creating content (like this book); however, the way we build this into my role and contribution to the organization is to make it like additional marketing material—like the cherry on top of what the marketing team are already doing. If I don't contribute or create anything, we still have a fruitful and thriving marketing engine in place.

Below, I explain each of the core areas of my role as I've defined them:

Vision

I see myself as the "keeper of the vision." I'm responsible for interacting with the vision, for holding it high so everyone can see it, and for regularly communicating it to my team, our investors, and our customers (and potential customers). It's my job to ensure everyone remembers what we're building, why we're building it, and how we show up each day in order to give us the best possible chance of getting there.

Essentially, this incorporates not only the *vision* (being the big goal of the organization) but also our *purpose* (the "why we exist" behind the organization) and our *values* (how we show up as a team culturally).

When I first realized I needed to bring these pieces to the forefront weekly in order for us all to stay connected with them, I started to jokingly refer to myself as Chief Repetitive Officer! Because it did feel repetitive. It felt annoying. It felt like we were all asking, "Why do we need to review this in every weekly meeting?" But in reality, if we had gone over it once, then put it away, then, over time, we all would have disconnected with it, resulting in us getting into the rut of *doing*, rather than *being*.

The days would become a series of tasks and projects, rather than the exciting life-changing work we were actually doing.

One of the other things I do for myself is create a personal vision statement for the organization and my role in it. I email it to myself and, each morning after reading it, snooze it to pop back into my inbox at 8 a.m. the next day. This quick moment is a daily reset and reminder for me of what I'm privileged enough to be working on and bringing to life.

I'm also always *listening* to where the company wants to go. I mentioned "I'm responsible for *interacting* with the vision," which means developing an energetic relationship with it, and through the practice of meditation and contemplation, it's my job to stay as open as I can be to receive downloads, instructions, or ideas about how the company may wish to evolve.

Strategy

It's my role to develop the bigger picture strategy for bringing the vision to life. This includes using strategic planning to integrate any of the ideas that come to me along the way. I see my intuition and that energetic relationship with the consciousness of the business entity as the direction we're headed in, and then I tap into my business experience and knowledge to develop effective strategies to get there.

I'd also liken this to the balance of the feminine and masculine energy within me as a leader. The feminine being this more intuitive, fluid approach to decision making, and the masculine being harnessed to bring everything to life through strategy and planning.

While I'm connected with my intuition, I'm also a data and strategy nerd. Through my experiences, however, I've discovered that starting with my gut feelings and then using the numbers to validate my ideas and to help inform the strategy is what works best.

Ironically, I learned to trust my intuition the hard way through the repeated experience of not following it, only to look back later and reflect on the fact I "knew" the way to move forward but had followed a seemingly more logical path instead. Eventually, this learning the hard way got through to me, and I began the practice of listening in, and then following what came to me even if it meant some shorter-term pain or uncomfortable conversations.

The more I practice this approach, the clearer this energetic channel becomes, and, in turn, appropriate strategies for execution come to me clearer and faster too.

Leadership

This part of my role is simple. It's bringing the above two pieces to our team, communicating it to them, and guiding us all in a collaborative fashion along our journey. Coaching, mentoring, and empowering everyone to bring their fullest potential to the table, through trust and candor. Leadership also takes the form of various meetings and communications, on an ongoing rhythmic basis, as is most appropriate. It's about monitoring and maintaining an expansive energy within the organization (this extends to team members, clients, remote professionals, investors, and any other partners or stakeholders). This translates to navigating into relationships with those who are aligned, and out of relationships with those who are not, as quickly and transparently as possible—aiming to hone one's skill (and tools) of discernment in this area to avoid entering ill-fitting relationships as much as possible.

This is where I thrive, and it's of course a practice to stay in my lane. Having discovered these three areas to be where I'm most expansive, creative, and powerful—essentially in my fullest potential because I both love doing them, and I'm good at it—it's my job to be vigilant with myself about sticking to them. Another term I've learned and like to use to describe being in our fullest potential is our "zone of genius." This is the intersection of what we're excellent at and what we love to do. A telltale sign of our zone of genius is the things we find ourselves doing that bring on a "flow state."

Flow state is the physical state we enter when we become unaware of the world around us, of time, and are completely engaged with the task at hand. Our inner monologue ceases and we become one with the moment. This is true presence. These are the moments we've expanded energetically into all we can be, and all we are capable of.

This is where we are most effective and powerful, where we achieve the most and have the greatest impact. However, it is not easy to achieve this state, or stay in it.

As founders (and I'm sure for leaders of any team), it's common for us to take things that sit outside of our role, simply because we know we can get them done, and to jump in and start working on something just to get it completed because we have the capability. Our capability, however, is not the point.

There are times we may *have* to step out of our roles and into other areas of the business, perhaps because the company is small and not fully resourced yet, or it's grown quickly and resources haven't scaled to match. When this happens in my own business, my focus is to step in for the shortest amount of time possible, by finding new team members or technology or empowering/upskilling existing team members as quickly as we can.

And before I decide to step into something else, I fully question our options. Why? Because while I may be highly competent at something (and I know many entrepreneurs will resonate with being competent all-rounders), it's *not* my zone of genius and therefore it won't see the company thrive. It is a survival tactic, and I want to spend as little time as possible in survival mode and as much time as possible in thriving mode.

Beware the ego

Our egos have a sneaky way of holding us back and will often be driving us into this behavior of working in and on things that are outside our zones of genius.

How? And why?

Fear of failure and fear of success. A need to be validated and seen as valuable, worthy, and enough. Guilt at having others do things we're capable of doing.

Let's dive into this a little deeper.

Fear of failure and fear of success

If our souls are love, our egos are fear. When our egos are driving the metaphorical car, it's from a place of fear. Our ego would rather stay safe, which translates to staying in our comfort zone and playing things out in a way that provides more certainty of the outcome.

Have you ever heard yourself say, "I'd rather just do it myself so I know it gets done, or so I know it gets done right, than have someone else attempt to do it and mess it up"?

This is our ego.

This is fear talking.

There are several risks to our ego when we stay in our lane and stop getting involved in other areas of our businesses. One risk is that mistakes will be made, or that things won't be done on time or to completion. Our egos can see this as "failure," and if we're attached to the business as an extension of ourselves, we might even feel this as a *personal* failure.

When acting from a more conscious place, we can perceive this as natural and normal, as challenges and learning experiences for growth. And, provided we don't step in and play savior (another of our ego's favorite roles) and we allow our team members to solve their problems themselves and clean up their own mess, the entire company benefits from the learning.

Another risk to our ego is that our team outperforms our expectations or does better than what we would have done. While this is something most entrepreneurs will lament they're looking for, the truth is there's a little ego death occurring when this first transpires, and it'll only start to happen when we're ready—when we're ready to allow others to be better than us at things, and to not feel threatened or inferior by this.

A need to be validated and seen as valuable, worthy, enough

If we have a tendency to swoop in and save the day, it's important to examine the reasons we may be doing this.

Every time we have to "fix" something, our ego feels validated and valuable. We perpetuate a story that without us, everything would fall apart, which of course makes us feel important and gives meaning to our existence. On top of this, because it's other people's problems we're "fixing," we can tell ourselves we're better than them, and also that we're of service, we're sacrificing ourselves to help others. We embody the savior or martyr archetype.

In fact, what we're doing is holding both us and them back from stepping into our fullest potential, from moving through the discomfort of challenge and expanding. At the same time, we're effectively constraining the growth of the company.

Our ego will constantly constrain the growth of our companies and get in the way of it becoming its fullest potential, until we wrangle it.

Guilt at having others do things we're capable of doing

Finally, many of us experience guilt when delegating work to others. Especially early on, when we build our first team, it can be extremely confronting to be OK with giving others work, work we know we're fully capable of doing ourselves. This comes down to a sense of worthiness. Who am I to think I can build something bigger than myself? Who am I to think I'm good enough/worthy? Who I am to step up and lead another? Perhaps the better question to ask is, "Who am I not to?" which reminds me of one of my favorite quotes of all time:

"Our deepest fear is not that we are inadequate. Our deepest fear is that we are powerful beyond measure. It is our light, not our darkness that most frightens us. We ask ourselves, 'Who am I to be brilliant, gorgeous, talented, fabulous?' Actually, who are you not to be? You are a child of God. *Your playing small does not serve the world.* There is nothing enlightened about shrinking so that other people won't feel insecure around you. We are all meant to shine, as children do. We were born to make manifest the glory of God that is within us. It's not just in some of us; it's in everyone. And as we let our own light shine, we unconsciously give other people permission to do the same. As we are liberated from our own fear, our presence automatically liberates others."

—Marianne Williamson
A Return to Love: Reflections on the Principles of "A Course in Miracles" (United States: HarperOne, 2009)

Understanding the drivers behind why we wouldn't just stick to our zones of genius is important; in fact, understanding our drivers is key to leading with consciousness. Rather than forcing behavior change, when we can understand the basis of why we do what we do, our behavior naturally changes.

I'm not, by any means, perfect at all of this. It's a continuous process and something my team and I talk openly about in our team meetings. Ensuring we're all roughly staying in our lane while making space for healthy contribution and collaboration.

CHAPTER SEVEN

BRINGING OUR
WHOLE SELVES TO WORK

In early 2017, I went through a divorce. In late 2018, I experienced a breakdown. I spent much of 2019 working on my inner world and exploring healing modalities such as the plant medicine Ayahuasca.

I kept my team updated every step of the way. Nothing was off the table. Well, the only thing off the table was *me* during my breakdown. I couldn't do anything, and I let them all know. I needed time out, and I had no energy at that moment to even care whether my company survived or failed, so I just asked them to do their very best. And I thanked them in advance for it.

The thing I've learned about bringing my whole self—and everything that's going on for me—to my team is that it gives them permission to do the same. We build deeper relationships and a loyalty that's fierce and true.

I'll never forget what transpired during that time. My rock bottom hit over a weekend when I'd flown back to Australia for a girlfriend's bachelorette party.

I was in an incredibly challenging romantic relationship that was pushing me to my absolute limits. I'd been in and out of high anxiety and bouts of depression over the previous months, and the long flight and proceeding jetlag was the straw that broke the camel's back.

I didn't sleep at all the night after I landed, and I forced myself to socialize during the winery luncheon to celebrate our bride-to-be (my gorgeous friend, Dani Wales). When we arrived back at the Airbnb we were staying at to get ready for a group dinner, I cracked.

We walked in the door and I collapsed in a heap. Thankfully, Dani understood exactly where I was at and promptly got on the phone to my sister. Together they arranged a flight for me to Hobart, Tasmania, the following morning.

I arrived at my sister's Sandy Bay home an absolute shell of my former self. All the holding together I'd been doing over the past six or so months was nonexistent, and I could barely speak, let alone run a company.

Everything I had on the calendar, I cancelled.

My beloved annual volunteer trip to Cambodia with Project Gen Z. Bali with my girlfriends. A speaking gig in Sydney. All of it. Cancelled. Running my company. Cancelled. Being a friend. Cancelled. For once in my life, I had no choice but to exist only for myself.

In place of all the "stuff," I chose to be still and figure out where I was at and how I could start the long climb out of the hole I'd gotten myself into.

Looking back, I think the unravelling started very slowly when my dad died in May 2013, and many of my current team were with me during that period too. Sometimes I think they knew before I did and saw it all coming, because the way they stepped up and offered their support and love and strength was awe-inspiring and overwhelming.

In fact, it was their response to it all that gave me full permission to take care of myself and do what I need to do, and for that I'll be forever grateful.

Up until this moment in my leadership journey, I'd still been trying to be strong for my team and had been putting on a little bit of a front.

But no more. There was no more front left in me, no more fight. And this gift of surrender was the greatest gift I've ever received as a leader.

It allowed my team to wrap me in their arms. It allowed me to step into my truth fully and wholly. To be all the things and let go of the idea I needed to be "responsible" for them, to be a guide, to set an example. Instead, I realized I am of them. We are one. And walking side by side.

It's not been the same since. In the best ways.

My teammates are my friends, and given how much time we spend together (even in a virtual context) this makes perfect sense to me. I'd much rather enjoy the connection I have with the people I'm building things with than to treat each other as robots.

It's normal for me to get on the phone with someone and for us to start talking about a client issue or a process we want to improve but then to somehow end up discussing tantra, or plant medicine, or some other thing we're currently interested in.

I love it. I love the diversity it brings and, more than anything, I love the connection it brings.

I want to be able to be there for a teammate in an hour of need, and I appreciate the people around me who've proven they have my back when I'm moving through something too.

It makes the work we do feel more meaningful and enjoyable, as I get to do it each day with some of my best friends.

CHAPTER EIGHT

A TEAM OF OWNERS

Around the middle of 2017, I was in San Francisco and Silicon Valley for a couple of weeks with The Hacker Exchange as their entrepreneur-in-residence. The Hacker Exchange was founded by a good friend of mine, Jeanette Cheah, and runs programs multiple times a year bringing entrepreneurship and business students from Australia, to start-up hubs around the globe.

At the time, Wealth Enhancers was a well-established business turning over just short of a million dollars in annual revenue. We'd been stagnant, however, in terms of any form of growth for the past four years. We just couldn't seem to get ahead.

With three financial advisers in Australia, all on salaries, yet not fully maximized in terms of their client load, it didn't make any sense to grow the team, yet the client numbers didn't seem to be growing at any significant rate either. I knew the model wasn't quite right, and I was doing everything I could to figure it out, primarily focusing on our lead generation strategy, which we had been making significant headway with.

I remember exactly where I was, sitting in Covo (the coworking space we were using), when I received a message that would change the way I engage and build my teams forever.

It was from one of my best friends, Freya Savage, who also happens to be the first person I ever hired back in 2009 when I was still working

41

in my family business. She was at university and came onboard in a part-time capacity while she finished her financial planning studies.

She'd worked with me for a couple of years before spreading her wings in the corporate finance world and was presently finishing up a year-long hiatus of travel around southeast Asia.

Her message was asking my opinion whether I thought she should renew her CFP. She'd worked long and hard for it, but knew she'd never be back in Melbourne working in a grey office building for a traditional financial company ever again. She wanted to spend more time in Bali; the city life wasn't for her right now.

Instantly, a lightbulb went off in my head.

Wealth Enhancers was already a fully remote organization, and our client meetings and everything else were already being held online. There was nothing saying our financial advisers needed to be in Australia, or in any one location for that matter.

My intuition was telling me there were more people like Freya, who loved and enjoyed working with people and in financial planning but did not want the typical nine-to-five office arrangement. My intuition was telling me they wanted freedom and flexibility and would be willing to be paid in a different way in order to have this.

A fee share arrangement, in place of a fixed salary.

They could work to bring on as many or as little clients as they wanted, and we'd split the fees with them, using the portion that the business kept to support them with training, systems, processes, administrative, and paraplanning support, along with marketing, and lead generation.

It'd be exactly like being employed, all working as a team toward the same thing, but they'd have more flexibility in terms of their workload and earning capacity.

I knew the entrepreneurial flair that existed in all the millennial financial advisers in Australia—I mean, I was one of them. Yet I also knew first-hand the challenges of starting and building a financial planning company in what had become an incredibly regulated industry.

I ran the idea by Freya, and she immediately jumped at it. I then threw together a simple survey to test my hypothesis and posted it up in the XY Adviser Facebook group (a bustling online hub of younger finance professionals).

With around fifty responses in twenty-four hours, my gut feelings were confirmed more than enough for me to start working on this.

I went into what's now been dubbed "Beast Mode" by The Hacker Exchange crew! I stayed in each evening, building financial models, talking with potential investors, and creating pitch decks. I was completely alive with this concept, and knew in my heart I'd found the missing piece of the puzzle.

As I built out the fee-share remuneration structure for the financial advisers, I was thinking more and more about the survey results. It was clear to me how much people valued a sense of control over not only their days but also their destiny. The idea of being able to build as big or small of a client book as one wanted was very well received. It was also clear to me how important ownership was, or feeling as though they were building something meaningful, rather than just turning up each day for a paycheck.

The idea of carving out a portion of the company's equity for my team seemed like a good one. Initially, I thought I'd maybe do it just for the financial advisers, the income generators, but quickly felt into what it would look like for everyone in the team to be a part of the equity pool.

A team is called a team for a reason—everyone's role is different but equally important in bringing everything we're working on to life.

Then and there I decided to carve out 10 percent of my company to the team. Equal parts equity (for when the company ultimately sold) and quarterly profit share distributed in the same proportions along the way.

All these changes, though exciting, were significant, and the first step was getting my existing team onboard. If they weren't for it, I'd ethically have had a hard time implementing it as I'd engaged them under a different type of arrangement.

I needed to ensure this was as good for them as it was the company and that we'd all benefit in the long run.

Pitching to my business partner and my existing team was my first step. After some backward and forward, questions, tweaking, and working together, we had something we were all excited about. It was go time.

Freya joined the company as our first new financial adviser engaged under this unique model, and by the end of 2017, we had a total of six financial advisers trained up and working with us (up from three). Revenue had increased by 57 percent, and we'd distributed profit to the entire team once.

We also had a pipeline of young and incredibly talented financial advisers who were really excited about joining Wealth Enhancers.

We'd launched the WE Academy where we were training external financial advisers from all over Australia on everything we did in our organization. As Australia's first and probably only purely millennial-focused advisory firm, the industry was certainly engaged and interested in what we were doing and how we were doing it.

Internally, our culture was thriving. With a fully flexible and fully remote team who all had ownership over this thing we were building, happiness scores were high, and turnover was low.

This was a breakthrough moment in my leadership journey. First, I'd not given up. Four years of stagnant growth and I'd kept at it, turning over every rock looking for the thing that would make the difference. And second, I'd trusted my intuition. This was the big one.

There's a Beyonce quote: "If there's one thing I'm willing to bet on, it's myself." I felt those words to the very core of my being. I had zero doubt in my ability to bring this all to life.

I don't think I'd ever believed in myself more fully than I did at this time, and that feeling of knowing and trusting my intuition so deeply opened me to a new way of being. I committed myself at that point to continue to deepen that connection, to trust what I'd always felt inside, and to f*ck the doubt and fear right off.

Fast forward to the end of 2018, and while the business was growing and going incredibly well, my working relationship with my now ex-husband, Finn Kelly, was not.

With this newfound level of trust in my own abilities, I felt as though I was driving with the handbrake on. We were butting heads on everything, and far too much energy was being spent defending my strategy and position.

After several months of negotiations, we came to an agreement that he'd buy me out of Wealth Enhancers, and as part of the deal I'd take on Grow My Team, our fledgling and struggling remote staffing business.

Once the dust settled on the deal, and I was ready to step into Grow My Team as CEO, it was time to connect with that intuition again and bring forward all my learnings from Wealth Enhancers.

I immediately put a 10 percent equity and profit share arrangement in place, and while we've only distributed profit two quarters since I took over, it was a pleasure to do so each time.

It feels good to know we all have ownership in this company, me as the CEO and founder, all my teammates, and now the investors who've backed us and believe in the big picture of what we're creating.

There's a special dynamic created when we as owners let go a little, open up, and bring people in alongside us for the ride. It also creates an energy of abundance, the opposite of the energy of scarcity that can show up when we're holding on tightly and fiercely protecting what we "own."

It feels good to me that all of us who are supporting Grow My Team to be all it can be will be rewarded financially both along the way and into the future.

CHAPTER NINE

CARRY YOUR OWN BAGS

I've been a member of the global community Entrepreneurs Organization (EO) since 2013. It has shaped a great part of who I am as an entrepreneur and as a person.

One of the things I remember most from my early days of joining, was the message that this is a "carry your own bags" organization. Another way to frame this would be "own your own experience," and what it essentially refers to is taking responsibility for how your experience as a member is within the organization.

We hear the term "awakening" or referring to someone as being awake. Being awake and aware of self is being conscious. Awakening is the moment in time or event that happens when we realize everything is happening *for* us, not *to* us, and that we have the choice as to how we respond to it all.

It's the realization we can create our lives exactly as we want them. We are never trapped in any situation or circumstance. We can change it. Even in the event we were physically stuck somewhere, we always have the power to change our inner world and therefore how we experience what's happening.

It's the awareness that what we believe is how we experience our reality, and the knowing that we can change our thoughts, therefore changing how we experience our existence.

As I understand it, some of us experience a grand awakening—a profound and often jarring moment where we wake to everything in our lives. In my experience, awakening has happened in stages.

My first recollection of understanding I had the power to create and change my reality was at the age of nineteen. I'd returned home from a six-month stint living in London and backpacking around Europe. Along the way, I'd overspent and arrived home to Australia in debt and stressed about it.

It would keep me up at night, feeling sorry for myself, and feeling like a victim. I felt trapped and like I'd never get out of debt and never have any money. I've been writing and journaling for as long as I can remember, and upon reflection, it was this practice that snapped me out of my bullshit.

I'd subconsciously created a story that sounded good whenever I wanted to talk about my money situation, which was often because it was stressful and on my mind.

The story went something like, "Oh my goodness, I just checked my bank account and another charge has come through on my visa debit card. I can't believe the bank lets us overdraw our accounts when we have no money in them, and it's ridiculous how long some of these international charges take to show up. How could I possibly keep track of all this? And now I've unknowingly overspent by a few thousand dollars!" (I can't remember the exact amount, but it felt like a lot to my nineteen-year-old self working $10-an-hour jobs.)

I was blaming the bank and the function of the Visa debit card for *my* overspending. I was blaming the bank for *my* poor practice and process of keeping track of how much money I had in my account.

I was stating that the bank should be responsible for my financial situation.

Not only was none of this true, but also it was energetically giving away all my personal power.

I'd lamented this woe-is-me story over and over, because it meant I could talk about it and express the frustration, fear, and negativity I was feeling without needing to take personal responsibility. I could hear back what I wanted to hear, those around me agreeing with me about how tough my situation was and how irresponsible the banks were, allowing young people to get in debt like this.

For the record, all this did was keep me stuck in my little pity party.

Then one day I was journaling about it all, and as I was writing, I witnessed my own words. When I write them down in my journal, which is a place only for me, no one else reads them. No one can respond to it, there's no validation or feedback, and in that moment I saw the truth behind the story.

Of course I knew the Visa debit card would allow transactions to go through even when the account had no money in it—the teller had actually warned me of this a year earlier when I'd set up the account. Whether I agreed with that being a helpful function or not was irrelevant. I knew.

Of course I knew I was overspending. In those days, I roughly knew of every dollar I had because I had so few of them. I absolutely knew I couldn't afford the shopping spree I'd gone on in Paris. You better believe I knew exactly what I was doing and didn't care because I was on a once-in-a-lifetime trip and wanted to enjoy the now and deal with the consequences later.

I saw my bullshit written out in front of me, and in that moment, I realized the only way out of it all was for the person who got me into it to create a plan and get me out of it. That person was me. It started and ended with me.

Damn. It was some tough medicine to swallow, but it was the best medicine of my life.

I created the mess. I can create the clean-up. I create everything in my life. Woah.

I stopped complaining about money, got another job, worked my tail off (I even pole danced for three months, but that's a whole other story), and paid that debt down. Once I climbed back to zero, I started saving and building wealth for my move to Melbourne because at the same time I realized I didn't like living in Brisbane anymore. With my newfound understanding of being able to create my own life and reality, I was in the driver's seat—making moves and taking charge!

With this early experience of waking up to my own power to create, the "carry your own bags" message within EO really resonated with me, and I was inspired by how my fellow members showed up each day and contributed to the positive and expansive culture of the organization.

It deepened my understanding of how we individually create culture and how we can positively impact the culture even when it may seem challenging. Everything we do has a ripple effect.

I reflected on my own early experiences working in teams where the culture sucked. Where we'd hit the bar on a Friday evening and spend the night complaining about work and our bosses and everything in between. I saw how we chose to put energy into *not* enjoying our workplace. We actually extended our displeasure by spending hours talking about the negative aspects of work during our time off!

Joining EO and the learning of this organizational value was a much-needed reminder of the power we each have to shape the culture of any group we're a part of (including humanity in totality, for that matter).

I mentioned earlier how in my first few years as a leader I'd complain to other entrepreneurs about how incompetent my team was. I'm ashamed of this now. It was my experience with EO that contributed to me deciding to start speaking my ideal team dynamic and culture into reality.

It worked. And it continues to work.

As the leader, I regularly remind my team, and talk it through with all new team members, of the concept we get to choose and create our culture—every single moment of every single day. We create our cultural experience by how we show up as individuals.

There are myriad places we can work in a team of people who hate their jobs, hate their bosses, and complain constantly about it. The only way to not *have* that experience is to not *be* that experience.

As the leader of our organization, all of that starts with me.

So that's what I do. I show up every day in truth and transparency with our team. I address challenges head on instead of lamenting and complaining about them. I talk openly with others if I feel a disconnect instead of talking about it to someone else. I use positive and affirming language and pick myself up and restate things when I slip up.

And while we can't ever control how others behave, my own experience shows me that when I show up to the world in a way I want to experience the world, it is my reality. I'm living proof of that, time and time again.

CHAPTER TEN

YOUR VIBE ATTRACTS YOUR TRIBE

I've long subscribed to the idea we're a reflection of those around us, and with intention, I have always gravitated to people who inspire me in some way. In my early twenties, I would constantly be making lists of those in my life and what in particular I found inspirational in them.

I wanted to always stay engaged with the positive aspects of a friend and remember why we were connected.

Since I was a teenager, I've had a strong connection with my intuition; however, I often found it overwhelming and hard to wrangle. I have often gone against it in favor of not rocking the boat or having a more immediate need met. I even spent years shutting it down and quieting the voice through busyness, alcohol, and the many other ways we humans develop to numb our connection with source and our higher selves.

What I've learned in more recent years—and continue to practice daily—is to listen and be in constant connection with my intuition. The inner knowing that always exists when we listen closely and open to it. When we are more in tune with it, it's easier to feel. For me, I experience it as a full-body feeling.

To me, it is energy.

I experience energy and energy exchange in one of two ways: expansive or contractive.

Every moment of every day, we're dealing with the energy of the world around us intermingling with our own energy. Whether it's another person, a group of people, a place, or even a concept—everything is energy.

What I'm listening to and feeling into my body for is how my energy feels in response to the changing energy around me.

Expansive energy feels clean, clear, and uplifting. It's complementary and raises our vibration or just general state of being. The words "clean" and "clear" are important as we can often feel raised momentarily and come crashing down quickly when we're not in fact in expansive energy but instead in contractual energy. It can feel overwhelmingly good, and then suck the life out of us. Truly expansive energy brings with it a gentler rising.

Contractive energy feels dense and lowers our vibration. It leaves us feeling tired, drained, and exhausted, whether mentally or physically. Paying attention even to the words we use to describe our state of being can be easy clues into how people, places, or situations are impacting our energy.

It's also important to note we can feel "exhausted" from an uplifting day spent doing and being something we love, but the exhaustion will feel different. It'll feel satisfying, and we'll still have an overall feeling of having expanded.

Likewise, we can have difficult conversations, but when we're in truth and the energy channel is clear, we can actually come away feeling expanded and revitalized.

As I've deepened my connection with my own energy, I've come to understand how to work with it effectively as a leader.

It's been a practice of addressing (whether internally or externally) the energy I feel head on. If I feel a team member is disengaged, I ask them how they're doing and let them know it's a safe space for them to communicate what might be going on. If I feel I'm disengaged, I'm honest with myself about that, communicate to my team how I'm feeling and why—if I know. If I don't know yet, I communicate that and let them know I'm diving into it to find out. Then I do that and follow up with them later.

This comes back to full transparency and trusting our feelings.

For many years, I denied my feelings if someone asked, because my ego rejected the idea another could see through my masks. I rejected the idea someone else could see more clearly my inner world than perhaps I could in that moment. Now, I get ahead of it. I just speak it, and if someone does ask me, I immediately get curious with myself about what might be going on that is showing up for others to see.

Much of working through this has been deconstructing conditioning around being right or wrong. Letting go of the black-and-white thinking many of us are raised to adopt.

It was a psychic reading that helped me understand all this in a new and relieving way.

I'd been referred to Teymara Wright through my Melbourne entrepreneur girl gang—a small group of inspiring women who show up every day for the world, their teams, and themselves. Whenever I'm in town, we get together for dinner and share our lives. This is an expansive group of souls!

A couple of them had been to see Teymara for a three-hour reading that included her putting together their astrological charts, numerology, and a tarot reading. I was in and managed to secure a spot that week due to a cancellation.

About halfway through my visit with Teymara, she looked at me and said with confidence, "You don't like being in Australia, correct? You don't like how you feel here, and you don't know why?" Instantly, I responded in affirmation.

For years I'd been trying to understand this part of myself that just wanted to be in the United States, and why I disliked Australia so much. It's a beautiful country, a safe country, a clean country, many,

many people I love dearly are there, but I just didn't enjoy my time there. I always felt off.

She explained to me that everything (and everywhere and everyone) has a vibrational frequency, and I'm on a different vibrational frequency to Australia. As simple as that.

This resonated instantly. It was a much simpler answer than what I'd been looking for to explain my feelings, and it was the beginning of me opening back up to my intuition and connection with feeling the energy around me.

What had been blocking me was thinking that if something felt off, it was "bad," and if something felt right, it was "good." I was resisting the idea that good or bad existed. Now I was free to see it as whether it's a vibrational match or not.

Prior to this understanding, if my energy didn't feel good with another person, I'd look for why they were a bad person to try to understand and justify my own feelings. Of course, what we feel about the world around us will only be reflected back to us, and I'd also find myself looking for the bad in me.

When it came to Australia, I'd always been wondering what was wrong with *me*.

Nothing was wrong with me or the beautiful land I was born in; I'm just going to energetically thrive more in the US and other places. I've always felt this way about certain places and of course used to frame it up as "loving" those places. But now I understand that when I land somewhere that's a vibrational match, I'll instantly recognize it and feel expansive. I feel this way in Bali, Guatemala, and Tel Aviv, and in all three places, I instantly knew I'd be spending more time there throughout my life from the moment I first visited.

Of course, everything is always in motion, evolving—people, places, and situations—so there's plenty of possibility for us to move into a vibrational match with things we were once out of alignment with. All we need to do is *listen* to how we feel.

Living from this place of understanding energy and vibration has been a great relief for me. Nothing is personal. Nothing is right or wrong, good or bad. And when I do find myself in an energetic mismatch, it's an opportunity for growth, for learning more about myself, for reclaiming my personal power and ability to choose my path, and for deepening the channel between myself and my intuition, my source, and my higher self.

I can feel into where my company wants to go with every opportunity that presents itself. I can listen and sense if it feels expansive or contractive. I can feel this with bringing on clients, partners, investors, and team members. It's all right there for me when I'm in touch with what's coming up for me inside and when I resist letting my logical mind rationalize decisions.

It was not rational for me to take Grow My Team on; it was never rational for me to keep the company going after losing money each month for two years and accumulating significant tax debt.

But I felt an energetic alignment to the vision, and thinking about where it could go eventually expanded me. I did fight with my logical mind several times; however (and thankfully), my intuition won out.

And ultimately since the moment I took the company over and moved into the role of CEO, I've never doubted anything. It's been a hard slog at times, but I've always felt connected to the bigger picture of what we're building. It has shown in the team we've attracted and built, our investors and our community of clients and contractors, and even more so now as we've expanded into the technology space with the launch of Growmotely—the world's first platform connecting remote professionals into roles they love with companies they thrive in.

I could never have known in January 2019 that in just fourteen months, the world would be thrust forward a decade in terms of remote work. The space we'd been playing in for six years—working to educate founders of the benefits of flexible work and diversity through global teams—become normal overnight as the result of a global pandemic.

As I closed our pre-seed investment round one Friday afternoon in early March 2020 to start working on the Growmotely platform, I could never have known that just a week later the entire world would begin a new way of working.

What I did know was that the energy of Grow My Team and Growmotely always felt expansive and drew me in. And that's all I ever needed to know.

CHAPTER ELEVEN

FINDING OUR RHYTHM

While some time ago we tossed out the idea of 90-day cycles, and that mode of business planning, it had served me well the ten years prior. Specifically, we had followed the Rockefeller Habits model, and then later merged that into the Entrepreneurial Operating System (EOS), sometimes referred to as Traction.

Both these systems were incredibly powerful and valuable. I can't speak more highly of them. They gave us a framework to follow, something to keep us on track and accountable. It was a tried-and-true process that we didn't have to figure out on our own, which meant we could plug it in and focus on building whatever we were building.

The way we operate now is unique to us. It has come together from all the practices we learned from the previous systems and the freedom and space we now have to listen and trust what is most beneficial for our culture.

As we get into some more detail of what and how we do things, I'll reiterate that these are our ways and not "the" way. This is where we've landed for now, and I have no doubt that we will evolve over time as everything in this world does.

In summary, this is what our current ongoing business planning, cadence, and rhythms look like:

1. Start with the vision.
2. Feel into the strategy.

3. Develop key projects/priorities.
4. Share weekly progress updates.
5. Deep dive into monthly data.

I'll explain each of these areas in more detail below:

Start with the vision

Every company I've started, I've done so because I feel called to solve a particular problem. An idea gets into my very being, and I can't shake it. I've developed some level of patience around this, because I also know how easily ideas and inspiration can strike; however, it's the execution of an idea that's lengthy, repetitive, and far more challenging. I wait and sit with it to see how truly obsessed I am, and eventually I'll either stop thinking about it or start a company because I won't be able to sit with it inside me any longer.

For those who've read Elizabeth Gilbert's book *Big Magic*, her description of the way ideas seek out people to bring them to life resonates most with me. It's as though they come and visit, and you spend some time together, getting to know each other to determine whether or not you're a good match.

I liken it to dating. You meet, maybe grab a coffee together, go for a walk. You see how it feels afterward and perhaps send some flirty text messages and see how they land. If you're both still feeling it, you go for dinner. As you get to know each other, you feel into whether it's a complementary fit. Is there enough intellectual stimulation? Passionate sexual chemistry? A heart-centered connection? How does it feel intuitively? Are your values aligned? Over time, you'll either become more and more excited about each other and dive into something, or you'll part ways.

That's what it's like for me when an idea visits. Part of the getting to know each other process is for me to explore where this idea wants to go, what it wants to become. I then check in with myself to see whether the path to get there feels like a path I'd enjoy going on, and whether where it wants to go is in line with my own personal desires for the future.

If so, it's on. Let's do this thing.

At that stage, I scope out, in words, as much of the bigger picture as I can get my head around and work to distill it into a vision statement, a purpose statement, and a set of values (all of which can shift and evolve over time as the idea is brought into physical existence). I tend to get a feel for the brand and what this company looks like "visually" at this point too. This early clarity is what seems to attract the right people into the vortex and before we know it, we're away.

Feel into the strategy

I mentioned part of getting to know the idea is to feel out what it'll take to reach the idea's vision or fullest potential and to check in with whether or not this aligns with my own skills, abilities, and desires.

This is essentially the strategy, which is also always in motion and can change; however, there will be a sense early on of what the strategy will entail overall and whether that piece excites me. Like I said, it's the execution that's far more challenging than the idea.

I'll spend time on pricing and build out two simple financial models. A start-up cost model containing the total budget required to get everything up and running pre-revenue, and then a basic one-to-three-year forecast to understand how long it'll take to get to profitability, what the cash shortfall will be to fund the initial losses, and what it will look like when it is in profit to ensure I can find a commercially sustainable model.

Personally, I don't ever create complex business plans. It comes together more as a statement of what it is we actually do (describing neatly the product or service), a vision statement, a purpose statement, a list of three to five values, and the two financial models—all put together on a slide show or document of some description in the company's first round of the branding.

That's it. And to me it always feels like just enough.

Develop key projects/priorities

Once the above two pieces are in place, we're now in the business planning cycle, which means continually reviewing all of the above and creating actionable key projects or priorities, as we like to refer to them, to move the company forward.

These priorities are larger projects that are not part of anyone's day-to-day role. They are things that, once complete, the business now has that thing and doesn't need to do it again. In the early stages, it'll be a lot of setting up specific systems and processes, developing branding and marketing materials, and establishing technology. As time goes on, these priorities will involve launching new pieces of technology, products, or services; reviewing how we do something; implementing ideas or feedback; etc.

One thing I came to terms with early on in my entrepreneurial journey is the never-ending to-do list. At first it was completely overwhelming, there was always so much to do, and it seemed I never got to the bottom of it as more things were being added by the hour. Literally. I'd be working away and get another insight into something that needed to be added or fixed and put it on the bottom of the list.

Eventually, I accepted it'd never end and that getting to the end wasn't the goal. Creating effective flow for the things on this list to be implemented was the most important thing, hence the development of key projects/priorities, assigned to someone in the team. As CEO I rarely, if ever, own a priority as implementation is not playing to my strengths or a part of my role. I do, however, contribute to priorities owned by others if and where my input may be valuable.

We use the term "priority" because it helps us all to remember this particular thing is a priority, and outside of attending to all one's regular day-to-day tasks, any priority we own needs to be at the top of our individual to-do lists. It helps us all make those decisions about where we need to allocate our time in a day quickly and easily.

For example, writing this book is a priority for me presently. It's one of the rare occasions I do have something on the agenda.

Another example of a priority I owned in recent times was our capital raise. Outside of items like this, our business priorities are owned by the team.

Anyone may bring a priority to the team as something they'd like to work to bring to life, and it's presented in our weekly meeting and agreed upon. The priority has a name, an estimated completion date, and a single paragraph description of what it is.

Generally speaking, the priority is owned by the person who brings it; however, at times we come up with a priority as a team through the open discussion that occurs in our weekly meeting. In that case, we'd decide on the spot who'd like to own it.

The owner of a priority will form a team around it (if needed) and together they'll work to bring it to life. The owner may do a lot or a little of the work, but they are most importantly responsible for ensuring it does get done. Each week in our All Company meeting, we go through each presently open priority and the owner of each will provide an update and bring up anything they're stuck on.

In the case of a "stuck" (which is what we call any friction point they're experiencing), we'll ask how we can help. Generally, we'll either brainstorm a solution together or someone will offer to help or solve the stuck. Often the stuck will be something they're waiting on, externally or internally. In the case of it being internally, it's a gentle reminder for whoever the priority owner is waiting on to keep moving.

Share weekly progress updates

Our weekly All Company meeting is the most important part of our week as a team. We're all on different time zones, and it's the one sixty-minute slot we all agree to be in attendance for. I look forward to this time with my team each week so much.

Because we're a fully remote team, we use Zoom and always have cameras on. It doesn't matter where you are or what you look like, we've all just agreed it's nice to see each other's faces. Because we're also fully flexible, it's perfectly acceptable for someone to be at the hairdresser, in bed, at the beach, or anything in between. The important part is showing up, not how or where you show up from.

A quick side story on this:

I actually did the first interview for Wealth Enhancers' Marketing Manager from the hairdressing salon. Theodora Gatin, who now works alongside me at Grow My Team, showed up to the meeting and I had my camera off. I warned her before I turned it on that I had a head full of foils and was sitting under the warming lights at Miss Fox in Melbourne. We both burst out laughing when I did turn my camera on. Needless to say, this kind of thing sets the tone and precedent for the fully flexible nature of our culture.

If anything, it's part of the experience getting to see each other in our different local environments, taking a break from doing something we love. Meeting family members, pets, or friends as they walk by the screen is always enjoyable too. It really is the embodiment of "bringing your whole self to work."

Our weekly All Company meeting follows a set agenda, and we use an ever-evolving Google Slides file that gets updated each week by anyone in the team who needs to update a section. As CEO, I host the meeting and screen share the slides so we're all looking at the same thing.

The agenda currently looks something like this:

- Review of our ***Vision, Purpose, Values, and Brand Promises***. We share examples of where we've lived out these things or where we've fallen short over the past week.

- During the writing process of this book, I've added a section called **Weekly Refresher** where we focus in on something in particular as a refresher. Could be a system, process, aspect of our culture, concept, etc.
- A volunteer reads our **Cheers for Peers** aloud, which is a list of shoutouts team members have given to other team members throughout the week for a job well done. A way to say thanks or acknowledge one another.
- Our operations manager dissects our high-level **Numbers** for us. We cover the financial position and other key metrics. This is a chance for us to ask questions and check in with how we're tracking overall.
- We go through each **Priority**, and the owner provides an update of where they're at and anything they're stuck on and need help with.
- The meeting ends with **Any Other Business**, a section anyone can add in anything to be discussed that doesn't fit anywhere else. Then we finish by briefly reviewing the **Action Items** from the previous week's meeting and any that've come up in today's meeting.

As with everything related to how we're operating as a business, this weekly meeting format is fluid. I mentioned while writing that I've added a new item into the agenda. This is an example of how we listen to the business needs and desires and allow it to naturally evolve over time.

Deep dive into monthly data

Finally, I have a standing monthly meeting with myself. I have two hours blocked out in my calendar to review all our business metrics, and while I'm regularly reviewing this stuff in different meetings with different team members, this meeting is a time to deep dive into it all myself. No distractions, just me.

We have a high-level dashboard that's simply a Google Sheet. It has tabs for each main area of the business:

- Financials
- Cashflow (90-day forecast)
- Sales
- Marketing
- Delivery (service standards)
- Happiness

I start here to get a high-level sense as to how we're doing, how the previous month played out in comparison to other months and in comparison to what we were expecting. I'll then use this high high-level data to dive more deeply into our various systems where I can find layers and layers of data and information.

As I go, I make notes: Things that need to be improved and attended to simply around the way we're tracking and recording data. Strategic ideas and insights coming to me as I move through it all. Areas I may need to consider as either new priorities, or simply things I want to set some time aside during the month ahead to focus on.

Anything actionable from these notes I'll assign as tasks in our workflow management system (currently Basecamp is the software we use to manage both communication and workflow for our entire organization).

While I certainly make space at the end of each calendar year personally to reflect on the year that was, and create vision boards, goals, and targets for the year ahead, for the most part, keeping the business in a constantly evolving and fluid planning state means we have room to achieve more than we thought possible.

We're never anchored to a plan we set for ourselves. The particular cadence and rhythms described above sees us moving forward more rapidly and achieving more year on year than we did before using more rigid planning systems.

This is what works for us.

CHAPTER TWELVE

TRUST THROUGH TRANSPARENCY

In January of 2016, I faced one of the biggest challenges I've faced as a leader. The previous two years had seen me overconfident in my abilities as an entrepreneur, and I'd thoroughly stretched myself.

I'd sold my first business, a private wealth management firm called WE Private, and was in the middle of a disastrous handover. I was at the beginning of a legal battle with the new owners, who were refusing to pay the second and third tranche payments (a balance just shy of AUD$1m).

Wealth Enhancers was about four years old, and we'd scaled up the team significantly, aiming to grow it following the sale of WE Private.

The League of Extraordinary Women was holding several large-scale conferences a year across Australia and some smaller-scale international events. We had a CEO in place as we worked to serve our growing community.

I'd also only just settled a two-year legal battle with my dad's former business partners, who'd initially offered the estate roughly $1,000 for his 33 percent share of Australia's largest non-institutionally owned financial services licensee. The business had tens of millions of dollars in recurring revenue and no debt. As the executor of the estate, I'd spent two years fighting these two men my dad brought into the business he'd originally founded. It was horrible to say the least, and given I had to act in the best interest of the estate and its beneficiaries, I was also bound to consider more than just myself and my own feelings.

In 2014, we'd launched Grow My Team, and in 2015, we'd launched We Love Numbers (a since-failed online bookkeeping business). We'd just had our first international retreat in the Philippines where we brought the entire teams from Wealth Enhancers, We Love Numbers, and Grow My Team together for bonding, sales training, and general business planning.

It was a hot evening. I was sitting at my uncle's place several hours outside of Manila. We were under the cover of his open-air outdoor living space (essentially a concrete slab with a roof, surrounded by palms, jungle vines, and plants of all descriptions), finally cooling off from the days heat, fans blasting at us from every angle trying to enjoy a cold beer with Pam, who'd been my right hand in business since she moved to Australia in 2013.

"Trying" because we were stressed out, and every conversation we had circled back to the state of our team at Wealth Enhancers, the cash position of the business, and how on earth we could pull this all off.

Finn was running We Love Numbers and was in the midst of a capital raise. We'd also contributed several hundred thousand dollars in start-up capital the company was using to operate.

Grow My Team was operating at a small profit and was being taken care of for the most part by Karyn Lurie, the general manager we had in place.

It was Wealth Enhancers that was the issue. We were bleeding about $100,000 a month, and the business already owed Finn and me about half a million dollars. There was little end in sight for this level of significant monthly losses, and once again we were sitting around discussing how much more capital we needed to contribute at that moment to pay upcoming wages and the mounting credit card debt.

Something hit me.

It was all such a front, and I was feeling like a total fraud. There was all this activity going on above the surface, looking shiny and bright and exciting, but the truth was I had two businesses that were barely breaking even and two that were losing substantial money every single month. None of these businesses were yet turning over a million dollars in revenue even, so the losses were proportionately significant.

We'd just flown twenty-plus team members from around the globe together for an international retreat . . . and sitting there that night reflecting back, I couldn't help but feel stupid. We absolutely could not afford to be spending money like that.

I realized in that moment that I'd been living with my head in the sand. A switched flipped, and rather than continuing to sit and complain about my team with Pam—an old pattern and habit we'd developed—I saw it for what it was.

My decisions.

My outcomes.

My problems.

Mine to fix.

If my team was not performing, I had choices. If my time was spread too thin, I had choices. If our strategy wasn't working, I had choices.

It was time to take my power back and start creating the future I wanted for myself and for my companies, Wealth Enhancers in particular.

I spent the next few days looking into just how bad things were. It was time for me to face it all head on if I wanted to change it. We went through our financials with a fine-tooth comb. Figured out every expense we could cut or reduce. We had honest conversations about each of our team members and terminated the ones who truly weren't the right fit. We worked on strategies for getting us back to a place of profitability.

At the end of all of this, no matter what we did, we were still going to be bleeding $30,000 a month, and there was nothing left for me to cut. Unfortunately, another mistake I'd made in this business was not paying myself a wage. So, I couldn't even reduce or pause my own salary.

I did a lot of soul-searching over those days until I knew exactly what I needed to do.

Up until this point, I'd subscribed to the idea my team didn't need to know about the financial position of the company or any high-level problems or decisions. This was partly because I felt it was my job to shelter them from the stress and partly because I didn't want them to know exactly how successful I was—or exactly how much I was failing.

Looking back now, I know all this does is create separation, and whenever there is missing information, we fill in the blanks anyway with our own stories.

I knew I needed to come clean. I needed to tell my remaining team exactly what had happened, where we were at, and what we were going to do about it. I also needed to ask them to take pay cuts for a short period of time in order for the company to survive. I needed to own the fact that I, and I alone, had gotten us into this mess due to my overconfident ego and avoidance of reality by keeping myself so busy and important I didn't have time to look at it.

It was one of the most challenging conversations I've ever had. I called a meeting, and we all got online. I let them know of the few team members we'd let go and why, I let them know the state of the company and what the months ahead would look like for us. I owned all of it. Through tears and regret, I apologized. I was humbled, brought to my knees, and I was deeply sorry.

I shared exact numbers and details around the poor decisions I'd made that had led us to this point. I spared nothing and laid myself bare.

I also presented our go-forward strategy with a conviction my team perhaps hadn't seen before. It was no longer blind optimism. It was a well thought-out plan, and I'd certainly found a fire within to rectify my wrongs and to get serious about bringing this company back in alignment with it's potential.

The hardest thing I did was share the fact that despite everything we'd been able to do, we were still going to be losing $30,000 a month, and I asked them all to consider whether they could afford to take a short-term reduction in pay. I assured them, whatever they were willing to reduce by, I'd work with them individually to build a target-based plan, in line with the company goals, to bring their monthly pay back up to its current level within six months.

I also gave them permission to walk away and asked them to each think about whether they wanted to come on this journey with me. I promised them I'd operate in a fully transparent manner moving forward, that I'd include in our decisions, but I pulled no punches in letting them know it was going to be hard work and we'd have to dig deep.

It was a somber meeting.

Made even more somber by the fact everyone had just returned home from our first international retreat. What a shit show.

After the meeting, and in the days following, I felt lighter. Deep inside, I knew I'd just significantly leveled-up as a leader. I'd done a very hard thing. I'd looked in the mirror at the darker sides of myself, and then put it on display for everyone to pick over.

While I was still feeling sick over the reality of it all, I was also feeling peaceful, knowing I had grown, and that we were now working toward something sustainable. I knew at my core it was the beginning of a new way of operating that would be more fruitful for us all.

Over the coming week, every single one of the team members on the call that day came back to me with a figure they could reduce their monthly salary by and a fierce commitment to walk by my side on our journey out.

Once again, I was humbled. Brought to my knees.

I'd messed up so badly, yet they were all willing to stand by me. Because I was human and I shared my flawed humanity with them.

I learned that week that transparency trumps all. Truth is the path to liberation, and I've not looked back.

We worked hard that year. I learned what magic exists inside of me when I have my back against the wall. The time also bonded us tightly, and our culture began to shift. This was around the same time I started asking my team how happy they were each month and stopped speaking negatively about them.

Within six months, we had managed to get everyone's monthly salaries back to their pre-crisis rates, and we closed the year out at only a small loss. I also started paying myself a modest salary. While our revenue hadn't yet greatly up ticked, we'd started focusing on the right things and preparing our foundation for the growth that did eventuate the following year.

This experience was also a reminder for me, as an owner and entrepreneur, to ensure I was focused on the most important thing.

When it came to Wealth Enhancers, I'd been focusing too heavily on revenue growth alone and loading up my team in the hopes that more people would mean more sales. Shifting my focus to profit and then diving into what was working and what wasn't meant we were able to grow more sustainably and sensibly.

It was during that year I identified the five key numbers and corresponding areas of the business that most heavily impacted our success.

1. Our marketing engine; specifically, number of leads generated monthly.
2. Our sales process; specifically, our percentage close rate.
3. Our service delivery; specifically, how efficient we were in number of days of attending to financial advice being implemented.
4. Our client happiness; specifically, the monthly happiness score and our retention rate.
5. Our culture; specifically, the monthly happiness score of our team members.

Over time, I became intimately familiar with these numbers and established a business metrics dashboard that enabled me to see these high-level numbers in real time. Whenever a number moved out of my determined tolerance range (too high or too low, depending on the metric), I'd dive into that area of the business and find out what the block was.

As an example, if our sales percentage close rate started to drop, I'd start poking around both deeper into our data (looking at individual salespeople) and also ask questions. Eventually we'd find the problem. By following the trail, using my intuition backed up by the questions I was asking, and looking at the hard data, we'd find the source of any issue.

It could be that a new marketing campaign, while still bringing in a high number of leads, was bringing in the wrong type of lead. It could be that a new salesperson needed more training. It could be something in our sales process, the actual conversation we were having with leads, needed tweaking.

Whatever it was, we'd find it and make adjustments.

This whole experience saw me absolutely loving my role as CEO of Wealth Enhancers. I'd found myself in my area of genius and able to stay focused on vision, strategy, and leadership. I learned a lot about myself and about how to most effectively run a company.

Looking back as I write this, it was January 2016 and that conversation I had with my team from my uncle's home in the Philippines that significantly changed me as a leader. It was that moment I became a more conscious and connected leader. My confidence grew and not the false confidence that comes with an overinflated ego. My understanding of how important it is to do our inner work deepened.

The change we wish to see in our companies, our relationships, our financial situation, the world, whatever it may be—that change occurs when we change from within.

The change comes when we ask ourselves the hard questions about our own role and responsibility within any given situation and when we do the hard thing with the answers we discover.

It seems to be that the only work that really matters is our inner work.

CHAPTER THIRTEEN

GOING INWARD

My greatest tool as a leader has turned out to be my practice of going inward, of reflecting on each challenge through the lens of self-responsibility and ownership. Asking myself questions like

- What role have I played in this?
- Am I proud of how I've handled it?
- What would I do again, and what would I do differently?
- Was there anything early on I ignored?
- What choices do I have now?

I do this by putting pen to paper, usually in my journal. I have always found a power in not just thinking about something, or talking with others about it, but in sitting with myself alone, contemplating deeply, asking questions, and writing out what comes to me.

There's an energetic transfer that occurs through the physical act of writing, and whatever it is we're mulling over both becomes clearer as we write with some form of inquisition and structure. We're literally moving the energy out of our body onto the paper, and as a result, we're no longer carrying the burden of whatever it is we're working through.

The same thing happens when we speak our truth and make space for the truth of others. Falsities muddy our energetic channels and result in us carrying the muddy energy around. When truth is spoken, the energy channel becomes clear and whatever it is can be more easily processed and released.

Being a leader, I've discovered, often means doing "the hard thing." Doing the hard thing is speaking into reality the truth of a situation and taking new and more aligned steps forward.

It is hard to be in truth. It's hard to sit across from someone who works for you and have an open conversation about a lack of alignment, to do this when you first notice it, and to hold space for navigating out of it. It may mean them leaving, it may mean changing roles, it may mean learning a lot about their traumatic home life.

But this is what it is to be in truth. It's raising things when you feel them rather than letting them fester. It's openly communicating, and creating a safe space for the open communication of others as we navigate the ever-evolving human experience.

It's reserving judgment when others are unable to share truth in the way you may want. It's reserving judgment of what their truth is. It's reserving judgment of what your own truth is.

It's communicating our own fears and doubts, along with our hopes and dreams, as they are in each moment. It's bringing all of ourselves to our team and company, without expectation of others doing the same.

It's being what we want to experience in the world, without expectation. Because all change starts within us. And our inner world is the only thing we have true power to change. There's a ripple effect when we trust and surrender to our truth and commit to speaking it. However, that ripple effect is something that will show up getting bigger and bigger over time.

Why is it so hard for most of us to do?

We've been conditioned from a very young age to hide and stuff down what we're feeling. Think of these statements:

- If you have nothing nice to say, don't say anything at all.
- You can't say that.
- Toughen up.

- Crying about it won't get you anywhere.
- Put on a brave face.
- What will people think?
- Don't be so sensitive/emotional.

The list goes on, and I'm sure many of us have heard these statements. They essentially say, "Who you are in this moment is not OK. Hide it. You are not 'enough' (or you are 'too much') as you are."

This subliminal conditioning results in many of us developing strategies to show up in the world how we think we "should." To say things we think are acceptable, rather than simply speaking our truth by sharing our emotions as they arise and being who we are in any given moment.

It's a practice to come back to center.

My journey back to center seems to have started when I left my marriage. Walking away from what I'd been conditioned to believe was the perfect life was one of the hardest things I've ever done.

My now ex-husband and I lived in an eight-bedroom, eight-bathroom mansion in Beaver Creek, Colorado, one of the most prestigious ski resorts in North America. We had successful careers, plenty of wealth, and all the right friends. While together we'd always challenged convention and certainly built the life "we" wanted, I'd been feeling the rumblings for a while that perhaps the life *we* wanted wasn't the life *I* wanted.

At the time, I was unpracticed at speaking my truth, especially to him. He's a person of conviction and a strong personality, traits that were both attractive and engaging to me for many years, especially when we were aligned in our thinking and what we wanted.

It was overall a very positive relationship; our energy was expansive, and we achieved a lot together, especially early on. However, I was noticing our ideas about life and what we wanted were starting to be different. As this became more and more apparent, it also became obvious I didn't know how to have my voice heard.

In the end, I left.

We went to therapy for several months, although by the time we got to that place, I was already checked out. It was frightening to me how quickly it was happening, and I did not have the tools to voice exactly what was going on inside me. It all came out as resentment and blame, and the only thing I could do at that time was exit.

I've spent years integrating that experience, reflecting in order to grow and grieving the loss of such a significant and transformative period of my life.

The biggest lesson I took from the marriage ending was I no longer wanted to live in any untruth, and for three years now I've been practicing clear communication (despite how uncomfortable it makes me). I have not been perfect. I've fallen into the old habit of thinking that I could manage my truth internally to not rock the boat, and, in those moments, I've practiced compassion for myself.

Over time, it's become easier and easier, and now I feel comfortable with the discomfort of sharing what's real. Writing publicly about the breakdown I experienced in October 2018 was a big step and was the beginning of the end of wearing any masks.

Take me as I am.

I quickly learned that actually meant *me* taking *myself* as I am, loving myself wholly and fully, and taking others exactly as they are— releasing expectations of how anyone should be and supporting them to be in their greatest alignment.

Friends.

Family.

Lovers.

Colleagues.

Everyone.

Be exactly who and what you are, and I will love you in that place, without conditions.

Everything I'm referring to here is a practice, and it's far easier said than done. However, like anything, with practice we become better and better at it, freeing the constraints one breath at a time.

And while these are personal stories, it's long been apparent to me that everything in our lives is connected.

When I grow into speaking my truth in my relationships, I grow into a place of comfort with bringing my whole self as a leader to my team, a place of comfort with sharing transparently everything going on in the business.

When I do work on my personal relationship with money, there's a flow effect to the way money flows into and out of our business.

When I'm physically fit and healthy, that vital life energy uplifts our team and the organization.

All the work we do on and for ourselves translates into us becoming more conscious and aware leaders.

Throughout this process, I've also become better at listening to my inner knowing, which ironically leads to fewer uncomfortable situations because we're able to move away from them early on.

Part of stifling our truth means stuffing down our intuition—not listening to the whispers until they become screams—and oftentimes waiting until a situation becomes so toxic it destructs in a fiery blaze of anger, hate, and blame. I guarantee in any of these big and difficult endings that if we looked back with compassionate reflection, we'd find that in that first moment when our inner voice said, "This is not the path," we ignored it because we didn't want to rock the boat.

This is what it's like when we hire someone we're unsure about or build a business we don't feel aligned with. The more time and energy we put in, the less we are willing to let it go and let others down, yet it's not right and it's never been right.

Listening to our intuition is a practice. Acting on our intuition often takes courage. But both become easier and easier over time.

I'm impulsive and excitable by nature, often jumping quickly ahead and into things before I've really felt them out. And I use the words "felt them out" in place of "thought them through" because likewise many of us become stuck in the decision-making process and move slowly as we're trying to use our rational and logical minds to make a decision.

In both cases if we take the time to quiet our minds and feel what's going on in our physical bodies, the path forward will become clear.

I've learned to put a little time and space between the excitement of now and the point at which I make any particular commitment or decision. This is because I know myself and I know how the initial energy of a new idea or partnership can feel intoxicating and enticing.

However, it may also have to do with the way I'm personally feeling that day or the momentum I may be having in other areas of my life. I've learned to sit with things through some of my own energetic cycles to see how the idea or partnership feels when I'm feeling tired, flat, agitated, or busy. I tune into how it feels in my body in different moments, and then I'll know whether it still feels good and expansive, or whether I'm feeling that contraction.

I honed this practice during the year or so I was experiencing depression. During that time in my life, I struggled to cope with what had previously been a perfectly acceptable level of activities, commitments, businesses, and projects.

It was fascinating for me to observe how, suddenly, I didn't want to go out and socialize or how I felt overwhelmed with a small decision in one of my businesses. Some days I didn't have energy to work. Things like posting on social media or writing my newsletter were practically impossible.

On days I felt good, I'd say yes to things at my pre-depression pace and rate. Only to wake up a few days later in the black hole and thinking, "Nooooooo, why did I say yes to any of this?"

One of the greatest gifts the experience of depression taught me was to slow down. To listen to my inner knowing. To create space in my life for me to be able to hear it.

Upon reflection, depression was a symptom of me not listening. I was experiencing increased anxiety after my marriage ended. I was diving into my new life with vigor and force and saying yes to plenty of things that weren't serving me in an attempt to escape the grief I needed to process—to avoid the inner work I needed to do.

I've since uncovered exactly when and why anxiety shows up for me. It's the tightness in my chest that shows up when I'm not living in alignment with my personal truth. It's my heart and soul letting me know I'm on the wrong path for me, for now. If I don't listen, the gentle squeeze becomes a vice-like grip around my heart and the center of my chest.

I was not listening in 2017, and by October 2018, the price of my ignorance had brought me down. Completely.

My increasing and relentless anxiety had turned to depression and culminated in me beginning to think thoughts of not wanting to live anymore. I caught myself before I became truly suicidal, and I caught myself because I know too well the power of my thoughts.

As soon as I observed the voice in my head saying, "I don't want to live anymore, this is too hard," I knew things had to change. Everything had to change. It was time to listen again to what I knew in my soul to be needed, no matter how hard those changes might feel. They weren't worth my life.

Climbing out of the darkness meant making a pact with my intuition that I'd start to listen to it, and to follow it. At first it was hard to hear, murky and contaminated with thoughts from my logical mind. But over time, and with practice, it's become a clear channel. At times I doubt it, and I struggle still with doing the hard thing that may come out of it.

However, the more I listen and slow down, and the more I act on my intuition, the easier it has become and the more evidence I've garnered to trust it. To know it to be my guiding light.

CHAPTER FOURTEEN

WRANGLING OUR EGO

Looking back over my entrepreneurial journey, I can see now just how driven I was in my twenties and into my early thirties to prove myself. Age is of course irrelevant; however, it is my own particular timeline I'm sharing. It just happened to be around the age of thirty-two that I reached a point where I'd achieved so much more than the lost and hopeless teen I once was could ever have dreamed up. It was time to rethink why I was doing all I was doing.

It was at this time in my life I unpacked the stories that had gotten me so far—one in particular.

My parents split when I was ten. My mum, my sister, and I moved away from our family home in Melbourne where I'd been born and raised and relocated to Brisbane. Immediately, my asthma improved and my eczema cleared up, conditions I'd suffered as a child that had led me to always feeling inferior and left out and missing a lot of school due to being sick and in hospital.

In Brisbane, with no past history, I quickly became one of the popular kids. This carried on through high school and was incredibly intoxicating for my ego. Finally, I fit in. I was in the "cool" group. I was considered attractive and, a few years later when boys and girls starting dating, I always had a boyfriend or guys asking me out. My girlfriends were the most popular in school, and the shy little girl I'd been was well and truly gone.

At the same time as all this newfound confidence was rising, I was angry as hell inside. Angry at my dad for leaving us, angry at the world for having our lives turned upside down, for the struggle I watched my mum face every day as we went from being a financially comfortable family to her having to work a demanding government job to make ends meet.

My internal anger and need for security at that age drove me to step into my masculine energy and to take on a father-figure type role for my mum and sister. I started working as soon as I turned fourteen (the legal age one can work in Australia) and did whatever the hell I wanted.

I was most certainly "off the rails."

I threw all the parties, did all the drugs, and, in all honesty, I don't know how I graduated high school with the number of days I skipped.

Needless to say, I had a reputation, and several of my friend's parents had either insisted or tried to insist they stay away from me. That stung each time I'd found out, not that I let it show, but, in the end, it was a teacher who really got to me.

It was toward the end of year twelve, and the Brisbane days in our public-school classrooms were getting hot and sticky. We had fans, but mostly no air conditioning, and not in this particular class. I don't know if it was the heat or the innately boring nature of the curriculum, but I was distracted, and as usual talking to whoever was sitting next to me. Laughing away, completely unengaged with the learning materials, and generally being a distraction to my classmates.

I found my report cards once and cried over them as I read over and over endless variations of "has potential, not living up to potential, easily distracted, a distraction to others." Years and years of them. All the same.

On this hot summer day, my teacher called me out. In front of the whole class, she asked me what I wanted to do when I finished high school. On the spot and feigning confidence, arrogance even, I quickly replied that I was going to study nursing at university.

In truth I had no clue what I wanted to do with my life, and I didn't particularly care. I had blurted out nursing because it's what my best friend at the time was going to do. She was clear and confident, so it seemed like a good idea to just go along with that.

Point blank, the teacher responded to me. "Nursing? At University? You really think you'd last a day at University? You don't have a hope in hell, Sarah, of becoming anything at all, let alone making it through a University degree."

Damn.

That moment and her words, along with every other disapproving adult's voice, became words and opinions I carried with me for the next fifteen-odd years. It cut deep, it hurt me to my core. While I almost believed her in that moment, that I actually was just a worthless piece of nothing, a little spark was obviously lit inside me at the same time.

That spark became the fire that burned on as I systematically achieved what the girl in that classroom never would have thought possible for her if she had believed her teacher.

My memory's a little hazy, but I'm pretty sure I told her to go f*ck herself and walked out of the room. This was the mask I wore back then. It was familiar, and it protected me big time from feeling my own disappointment in myself for being so unable to contain and control my inner turmoil.

How fascinating it was for me to discover this unique driver. I don't know whether to thank or loathe that teacher, because in the end it was that moment that drove me to everything that transpired in the years ahead.

In attempting to prove her, and everyone else, wrong, I ended up completing two diplomas, a bachelor's degree, and myriad shorter executive programs, and I ultimately completed the Entrepreneurial Master's Program at MIT in Boston. I paid my way through all of them without taking on debt, working full time as I studied part time or online, supporting myself financially since I was sixteen.

On top of education, I threw myself into business and entrepreneurship, along with financial planning and the not-for-profit sector. I won as many awards I could get my hands on to further externally validate my success. I was the youngest board member on the Association of Financial Advisers (Australia) board and held numerous other board positions. In my healthiest financial year, I donated $80,000 to build an early learning center in Bulgaria.

I mean, way to show 'em.

Eventually, however, I reached a point where I realized the accolades and achievements I'd been striving for were driven by fear. Fear of not being enough. Fear of the old story that I was worthless. All of the "success" I'd attained in my adult life had largely been driven by trying to prove myself.

When I stripped it all back, it was to prove to myself I was worthy, enough, and capable of anything.

This realization had me thinking, though: Every time I'd faced fears and overcome them, my life had exponentially improved. Every time I'd done something out of love and possibility, I'd felt the flow and reward both on the journey and at the pinnacle.

What if I could let go of the overall fear story that had been driving most of everything to this point career-wise and tap into love and possibility in its place? How would that feel, what might come of it? What was my fullest potential when I was operating from a more expansive energy? Operating out of a forward motivation toward what fulfilled me most rather than away from being worthless?

Once again this has been a journey—a journey of practice and a journey toward fully releasing the old story I need to be validated externally for me to be worthy and worth something in this world.

Along the journey, I've learned to check in with myself as to what my drivers are around any given situation.

I *became* an entrepreneur, and dove into the full experience of it, to prove I wasn't a failure. I'm *still* an entrepreneur because I love creating things. I love being the incubator of an idea and the steward for a time as it comes to life. I love building a team around me and challenging myself to create an environment for them to achieve maximum growth and success (whatever success means to them). I love the game of aligning myself, our team, our customers, and the way our company operates to make space for the brightest illumination of what the company was birthed to be.

What resonates with me most as I write this, and after much soul-searching, pondering, conversation, and contemplation—starting back in 2018 when I couldn't stop thinking about what it meant to reach one's fullest potential—is that our fullest potential as individuals is our greatest expression of what's possible in any given moment.

And our greatest expression is never fear based, because the energy of fear is contractual. Sure, it produces results, movement, outcome; however, it will always be a constraining and limiting energy. The energy of pure love and possibility is different; it's expansive, fluid, and evolving, and it fills the room in a way that lifts everything and everyone. That, to me, seems to be our fullest potential.

A peaceful undercurrent, an explicit engagement with the present moment, a feeling of being all we can be in this instant.

AFTERWORD

As I finish up this book, I reflect on both my life as a leader to date and on the adventure I embarked upon in putting all of these words, feelings, and thoughts together.

Like most everything else in my life, the idea to write this book came to me during a conversation. I sat with it for a few days, and once I felt both an intuitive yes and a clear, energetic engagement with the prospect, I started writing.

The conversation was with my now husband, Joe Hawley, one afternoon just a few weeks into the COVID-19 pandemic-induced lockdowns. Doing the final edits on this book, I'm six months pregnant with our son. Our relationship is unlike any relationship I've experienced previously. I'd call it sacred union—unconditionally loving, open and honest, expansive. We made a conscious decision together to be married on October 22, 2020, after finding out we were pregnant in July. It was the happiest moment of my life.

So much has happened since I wrote this manuscript, and I feel compelled to share it here—my final note, as I know with certainty that I'm at the early stages of the next chapter of my life. Or perhaps a better way of putting it is that I'm living though chapter one or two of the next book.

The Friday before the US announced we all needed to self-isolate, we closed a pre-seed round for Growmotely, oversubscribed by

32 percent. I took the extra funding, anticipating what may lay ahead economically.

Worth noting is I'd lost momentum on this, my first ever capital raise, over the winter months, with Christmas and the slower energy of the year end. Toward the end of February, I woke up in the middle of the night at my home in Keystone, Colorado. Tossing and turning for hours, I was having a hard conversation with myself.

What are you doing with this capital raise, Sarah? You haven't really touched it in months, we're only halfway to our target, we've started spending what we've received—but while it sits open, you're allowing it to drain energy and focus away from building the company.

I was so afraid I couldn't raise the money. I feared that the company wasn't as good as I thought it was crept in. I felt guilty for spending other people's money before closing out the round. You name it, every self-limiting, self-doubting thought surfaced.

I allowed them, I witnessed them, I wrestled with them, in moments I succumbed to them, in other moments I fought with them. I leaned into my process (it's not the first time I've woken up wrestling with something big) and eventually something wiggled free.

A compromise.

This cannot be the never-ending capital raise; I was firm with myself. And also, you cannot hand-on-heart say you've given it your absolute everything just yet. Set a date, give it one last red-hot crack, and close the round on the set date, irrespective of the outcome.

Next Friday, I decided.

Finally, I fell back to sleep. I woke up late the next morning, got myself a coffee, and went back to bed. From there, I sent messages, emails, Facebook notes, and Instagram DMs to anyone and everyone I could think of letting them know I was closing the round the following week. I ended up with five new interested investors. I met with them in the coming days, and by the following Friday morning, I had four new investors and closed our round out with substantially more investment dollars than we'd originally been looking for.

After months of no momentum (held back by my own fears), the moment I stepped up and into my destiny, the Universe greeted me.

Growmotely specializes in building fully remote teams, culturally matching growing companies with experienced and skilled professionals. Thanks to a global pandemic that's seen the entire professional world working from home, virtually everyone now understands what we do and why. Not only this, they've experienced the myriad benefits this freedom and flexibility can provide for an organization and their team.

As for most of us, the time of self-isolation provided me with space and quiet. My connection with myself and the energy of the world around me has increased exponentially. My connection with the business I'm leading has increased exponentially. This business is not me, and it is going to change the world. I know it with every cell in my being, so much so that I'm not afraid to write it here.

This is the bigger picture of what conscious leadership means to me. While I am not my business, or my team, or my awards or accolades, or my friends or family . . . I am also all of those things and more.

Every single thing in this world is an expression of everything life can be.

My work is to stay open and connected. To listen to my heart, my higher self, and the energy of the world around me. To allow all to be as it is meant to be, and to allow my own energy and alignment to flow as it is meant to be.

Embrace non-attachment.

Recognize and release resistance.

Contemplate.

Inquire.

Look within.

Remain open and always lean into possibility.

With an open heart and expansive love, I wish you every success as you embark on your own personal journey to conscious leadership. It is my hope for the future we all lead this way, building companies and teams that are both good for people and good for the planet, trusting the abundant flow of money as energy will follow this way of interacting with business.

—Sarah Hawley

ACKNOWLEDGMENTS

'm so grateful to my team, and to everyone who's ever worked with me, for being a part of my journey toward becoming a more conscious leader. It's not possible for me to have gotten to where I have without the mirror you are and have been for me.

ABOUT THE AUTHOR

Sarah Hawley is a serial entrepreneur and investor, having founded eight companies since 2009. Following three successful multi-million dollar exits, she is currently the founder and CEO of growmotely.com (the first global platform for sourcing, growing and leading remote teams). She's personally fueled by a passion for challenging the status quo of how we work, conscious culture and leadership, community, diversity and equality, and living life on one's own terms.

Sarah is a professional speaker and published author, appearing on TV and writing for many popular publications. She has also held board positions with several not-for-profit organizations including Project Gen Z, Project Futures, Entrepreneurs Organization, the Association of Financial Advisers and the Institute for Global Women Leaders.

Recognized as the IFA Thought Leader of the Year, Sarah was also named as one of Melbourne's Top 100 most influential, inspiring, and creative citizens by The Age, and listed in the Top 50 Female Entrepreneurs under 40 by Shoestring. She has completed the Entrepreneurial Master Program at MIT, holds a Bachelor of Business, and several diplomas.

Thank you for spending a some time with
me and my journey to leading from a
place of more self awareness.

I'd love your feedback on what chapters helped you most
and what you would like to see in future books.

If you enjoyed this book and found it helpful,
please leave a **REVIEW** on Amazon.

Visit me at

www.growmotely.com

www.sarahhawley.life

www.consciousleadershipbook.com

and sign up for email updates.

CPSIA information can be obtained
at www.ICGtesting.com
Printed in the USA
BVHW070809160621
609629BV00007B/737